Destined for GREAT Things!

Life's Trials That Bring out Seeds of Greatness in You!

~ ~ ~ ~ ~ ~ ~ ~ ~ ~ ~ ~ ~ ~ ~ ~ ~ ~ ~

Dr. Mia Y. Merritt

Morris Publishing
3212 East Hwy 30
Kearney, NE 68847

✹✹

i

Library of Congress Card
Number #2007904281
ISBN 978-0-9720398-0-2

Destined for Great Things!

First Printing August 2007

Library of Congress Cataloging-in-Publication Data
Merritt, Mia

Printed in the U.S.A. by
Morris Publishing
3212 East Hwy 30
Kearney, NE 68847
1-800-650-7888

ACKNOWLEDGEMENTS

I would be remised if I did not acknowledge the women who have been extremely instrumental in my personal growth and development. The ***Women's Master Mind Group*** of Miami, Florida has helped me to cultivate and nurture the gifts that God has imparted inside of me. Uplifting and encouraging each other through successes as well as failures has made each of us stronger spiritually, mentally, and psychologically. Thank you for helping me to realize that goal setting and planning are essential in acquiring success. I have learned from you ladies that I must have a personal affirmation for my life, clear and distinct goals that are written down, action plans, and target dates if I am going to manifest the desires of my heart in this life.

So thank you *Lawanda Scott, Juanita Mitchell-Dawsey, Gail Seay, Isabella Rivers-Bell, Alice Fincher, Tanya Jackson, Nifretta Thomas, Brenda Riggens,* and most of all I thank you ***Ann McNeill.*** Had it not been for Ann, her love, constant words of encouragement, motivation, and wisdom, I probably never would have begun to develop long and short-term goals and diligently work towards accomplishing them. Thank you for being my role model and most of all thank you for being my friend.

To my mother *Odessa Leanne Smith* and my three sisters
Lisa, Dori*,* and ***Chastidy & Tasha***

I love you with all my heart.

DEDICATION

This book is dedicated to my eight-year old son
Stephan Raynard Sanders.

I pray that you will walk in the Spirit of wisdom, integrity, and humility. As you continue to mature, your understanding will expand and the wisdom of the ages will be opened up to you. You will be limited in your understanding only by your unwillingness to abide by spiritual principles and grow. Always remember that the trials and tribulations that you will encounter in your lifetime are designed to make you stronger and bring out the greatness that is already within you. I pray that God will grant you favor in His sight. Remember to acknowledge Him in all of your ways so that He will guide you through your life's journey. He desires your praise & worship, so give to Him what is due unto His holy name, and He will never leave you nor forsake you. God will be with you always.

I love you sweetheart.

Mommy

In memory of my daughter,
Stephanie Leanne Sanders
Your Spirit will always remain alive
in my heart. I will forever cherish
the 93 days we spent
together.

God Bless You!

FOREWORD

The number "7" denotes completion. *Destined for Great Things!* was originally written in August 2002, but was not revealed for fear of what others might think and say. Since then, I have realized that liberty often comes through confession, and that through my story, others may be blessed, encouraged, and delivered. The time has come to reveal my life story to the world.

This book was inspired by two books that literally changed my life. Those books are, *The Greatest Salesman in the World Part I* and *The Greatest Salesman in the World Part II,* by Og Mandino. The chapter introductions in this book are derived from those two books with variations to some degree. I have simply augmented and modified concepts that parallel the challenges of my life. I thank God for the courage, faith, and wisdom to be able to write this book. Through the Holy Spirit, I have been able to bring forth a gift that has been inside of me. I thank God that although the revelation of this book was delayed, it has still been birthed.

Not everyone will tell their story, but everyone has a story to tell. I've decided to tell mine. By the grace of God, I have come through some difficult experiences. It is through my adversity that He has strengthened my character. It is through my challenges that He has helped me to stay on the path that leads to the unfolding of my destiny. To God be the Glory!

Mia Y. Merritt

CONTENTS

ix

CONTENTS

Destined for GREAT Things!

Life's Trials That Bring out Seeds of Greatness in You!

~ ~ ~ ~ ~ ~ ~ ~ ~ ~ ~ ~ ~ ~ ~ ~ ~ ~

Dr. Mia Y. Merritt

*C*hapter

1

Develop Good Habits and Practice Them Daily
Deliverance in the Midst of Praise

*A*s a child I was slave to my impulses; now I am slave
to my habits. My actions are ruled by emotions, love, hate,
appetite, environment, fear, anxiety and habit. The worse of
these elements is habit. Therefore, if I must practice habits, let
me practice good habits. My bad habits must be
destroyed and new fertilizer laid for good seed.

Both success and failure are the result of habit.
Successful people practice habits that failure minded people do
not like to practice. Good habits will never produce bad results.
Bad habits will never produce good results. Only a habit can
overcome another habit. In the beginning, I make my habits, but
in the end, my habits make me.

I will get into the habit of rising early, praying daily,
talking less, listening more, smiling often, and speaking positive
in all manner of conversation.

As I develop good habits and practice them daily, they
become a pleasure to perform. If they are a pleasure to perform,
it is my nature to perform them often. When I perform them
often, they become a habit, and I become their slave, and since
they are good habits, then this is good.

1

THOU SHALL NOT STEAL

B ad habits are easy to make but very hard to break. This fact became a personal reality when I began stealing. At the tender age of eight, I was introduced to shoplifting by my babysitter who kept me after school until my parents came home from work. I would go to the stores with her and watch her sneak things into her purse and pockets. I was also given the task of informing her if anyone was coming or looking. I had often seen her sneak money out of her mother's purse. On a few occasions, her mother would fuss about money missing from her purse, and my babysitter would accuse one of her three brothers. Their mother would blame one of the boys as well since they were mischievous. At nine, I began walking to the convenience store after school and stealing candy. When I was in the sixth grade, I began stealing quarters out of my mother's purse and soon thereafter, I graduated to dollars. When I grew into my teenage years, I was introduced to department store stealing. My friends and I would shoplift and take things such as clothing, makeup, costume jewelry, cassette tapes, but mainly clothing. During my adolescent years, I began stealing on my own without the company of my friends. The habit became such an obsession that I could not go into any store, gas station or office without stealing something – lipstick, perfume, lotion, gum, pens, notepads, candy, aspirin, you name it. This went on until the day my friends and I were finally arrested for shoplifting. Since I was then 18 years of age, I developed a criminal record. Unfortunately, it did not stop there. I continued to shoplift until I was arrested a second time. However, for some reason, I never stole anyone's wallet or took money out of anyone's purse other than my mother's. Deep within I knew that was totally wrong, although there is no better sin. I stole out of stores primarily. I knew that stealing out of stores was taking from someone indirectly, but I felt that whoever owned the store were rich, and I was not hurting them. Surely, I no longer think that way.

It was not until I decided to seriously learn about God through reading His Word daily that I was delivered from stealing. The funny, but mysterious thing about the situation is that I was not trying to be delivered from stealing. Learning about God and shoplifting were two separate aspects of my life. I was just curious about God and wanted to know what was written in that Bible. However, one day as I was reflecting over my life, I realized that I did not steal anymore. I had immersed myself into reading the Word, praying, fasting, and learning about Him, that I could not see nor feel the change that was taking place in my life. That is how unfathomable, yet powerful the Lord is. He is a gentleman. He does not force Himself on anyone, but He is faithful and willing to deliver us from all of our sins, troubles, burdens, and strongholds. Stealing was a stronghold in my life, but as I began to learn about my Father's business, He purged me from the things in me that were not like Him. The Word of God is light. Light and darkness cannot dwell in the same place. One has to be dominant. Therefore, as the light of God was entering me through reading, and as my spirit was being washed through fasting, and as my heart was being cleansed through prayer, the darkness had to leave. There is no happy medium with light and darkness nor good and evil. Anything that is not like God is darkness. Stealing is darkness because it goes against what God has commanded us to do. When I lifted my head up to look at my life, I realized that the stealing was gone, the urge to steal was gone, and the profanity that use to come out of my mouth was gone. God is just awesome. He has delivered me from all those bad habits. He is so faithful. In Him, there is no darkness!

TEMPTATIONS

Not stealing anymore was not without its temptations. I knew that I had been freed from taking things that didn't belong to me, but the temptations still came from time to time. There were instances when I would be in the store and had the perfect opportunity to steal something when no one was looking, but I did not do it. I knew that God was watching. Paying for everything that I brought home and refusing to give in to temptation was an exhilarating feeling. When the forces of evil realized that I could not be tempted in the usual way any longer, another approach was presented to me disguised as a so-called blessing. While paying for a few items in the grocery store one day, I handed the cashier a ten-dollar bill. She gave me change for a fifty-dollar bill. As she was counting the change back to me, I realized immediately that it was wrong. She handed me the money and began trying to scan the next customer's items. I discreetly told her that she gave me too much money back. I proceeded to tell her that I had only given her a ten-dollar bill, but that she had given me over forty dollars back. She was very appreciative and gave me the correct amount of change. However, I can not say that the thought of keeping the money did not enter my mind because I was low on cash and could really have used that money. Additionally, I could have rationalized keeping the money in my mind by saying to myself that it was a blessing from God, but God does not cause problems for one person in order to bless another. That young lady could have lost her job for being short in her register. I was very proud of myself when I left that store. The Lord did not give us the "Thou shall not steal" commandment just for our own spiritual discipline. He gave it to us because there is a power in resistance to temptation that crushes the enemy's head. It tears evil out by the root!

THE EXPENSIVE BRACELET

Yes, little temptations came here and there, but I passed every test. Once we resist the temptations presented by the forces of evil, they depart. Every now and then, new schemes are tried to regain entrance, but with enlightenment, comes wisdom and the ability to recognize those evil plots. The ultimate test that really confirmed that I was truly free from stealing happened during the Christmas holiday season. After being driven to my car by mall security after hours of shopping, I noticed a small JC Penney's bag sitting on the passenger seat of my car. I was very perplexed because I had not gone into JC Penneys and I did not purchase anything in a small bag. When I looked inside, it was a beautiful diamond tennis bracelet. The bracelet was in a gift box and the receipt was still in the bag. The cost of the bracelet was $289.00. Immediately, I became very afraid. I thought that someone was trying to set me up. Fear took over me. I looked around and drove home, terrified the whole time. When I arrived home, I called mall security because they had driven me to my car as I was leaving the mall. I thought that I had inadvertently picked up that little bag in the security vehicle that I rode in. But when the driver called me back, he said that there were no bags in the truck, and that he had just gotten the vehicle when he took me to my car. This was really a mystery to me. How in the world did this beautiful, expensive bracelet get into my car? After the security guard told me that it did not belong to him, I envisioned myself keeping it. I tried it on and it fit me perfectly. I have a very tiny wrist, and for the bracelet to fit me so perfectly, it had to become mine. I was soon led to call JC Penneys. I explained to the person on the phone that I had found a tennis bracelet that was purchased from their store and would like to know if someone had reported a missing bracelet. Yes, someone had. The young lady told me that a gentleman had called and wanted to know if he had left it at the counter after he purchased it. He left his phone number in case anyone turned it in. She took my number and told me that she would have the gentleman call me. She was surprised that I would be calling to turn in an expensive bracelet and told me that I was very honest. Ten minutes later, a gentleman with a heavy accent called me about the bracelet. He indicated that he had lost it, but did not know where he had lost it. We arranged for him to come over to my house and retrieve the bracelet. I told him that he would have to show me his driver's license and credit card number that matched the last four digits of the number on the receipt. I asked a friend of mine to come over as a precaution.

The gentleman came over and immediately I knew who he was and how he had left the bracelet in my car. He did not remember me, but I refreshed his memory. I had been driving around the mall parking lot for about 20 minutes trying to find a parking spot. I was so desperate and frustrated that I was about to drive back home. But then I saw an Arabian-looking fellow walking to his car. I rolled my window down and asked him if he was leaving. He told me yes, so I begged him to let me drive him to his car so that I could get his parking spot. He seemed a bit afraid at first (go figure), but he got in and let me take him to his car. When he got out, that's when he left the bracelet.

His credit card matched the receipt. His wife and baby were in the car and he motioned for them to come inside. He explained to me that they were celebrating their three-year anniversary, and the bracelet was a gift for his wife. The baby was a three-month-old little princess who was absolutely gorgeous. The wife brought me a token of appreciation, two long thin wine glasses. I played with the baby for a moment and then they left. Wow, talk about a 360! Who would have gone through all of that just to return something of so much value? only an honest person who had been truly and completely delivered from stealing. In Jesus, the greatest things that were once a weakness can become a great strength. He is the rock, the fortress, the deliverer; our God, our strength, in whom we will trust. Bless His holy name!

THE COUNTERFEITER

The forces of evil are counterfeiters. They have a counterfeit for every genuine reality that God has. He diligently works against everything that God wants to purpose in our lives. One example of this in my life is the fact that God's Word commands: *"Thou shall not steal."* However, the enemy of my faith tempted me into doing the very opposite of what God had called me NOT to do, steal. How does this happen? Because demonic forces are sent on assignment to tempt us. Whether or not we give in, is totally our decision and a decision that we must live with. The ultimate goal is to destroy us. The spirits are very subtle, tempting in small areas at first. The spiritual reality is that evil forces are sent to sift us as wheat. When something is sifted, it seeps out gradually until all of its contents are completely gone. The enemy of my faith wanted to sift me so that I would not realize what was happening to me until it was too late. By then, I would have been completely consumed. But God, in His mercy did not allow that to happen to me. He intervened just in time. I took the first step and He took the rest. Praise God for grace, mercy, and deliverance.

THE SPIRITUAL WAR

There is a constant, ongoing war occurring in the spirit realm and the more we deny it, the more likely we are to be used by the forces of darkness without realizing it. The first time I stole, a feeling of guilt and conviction overtook me. When I stole the second time, I felt less convicted, but I continued to steal, until I had very little feeling about it at all. What I did not realize is that each time I gave in to temptation, the spirit that was sent to tempt and destroy me grew stronger, making it much more difficult for me to resist. I became obsessed with stealing and eventually could not control myself. Nobody is exempt. The enemy continues to tempt in other areas as well, and if we submit to temptation, doors open for other demonic spirits to enter our lives until a transformation has happened for the worse. This is what happens to drug addicts, prostitutes, adulterers, and even murderers. If you were to ask them, they would tell you that they all felt guilty after their first offense, but each time they repeated the sin, those convictions diminished to where they were completely eradicated. Resist the enemy, and he will flee from you. Develop good habits, and practice them daily.

DELIVERANCE, PRAISE, & WORSHIP

As I grew in maturity and wisdom, I consumed myself in reading God's Word and the Word became life inside me. It became alive in my heart and soul. When I began reading and praying diligently, God took care of the areas in my life that needed repairing or obliterating. It was a liberating day when I woke up and realized, *"I don't steal no more! I don't curse no more!"* I am a witness and God is my judge that when you give Him your whole heart and focus on pleasing and learning about Him, He will purge and deliver you from everything that is not like Him. His visitation will become habitation. Whatever or whoever is exposed to the manifested presence of God, begins to absorb the very material matter of God. Once God delivers from demonic strongholds, resisting the flesh and walking in the spirit is a must, otherwise, the deliverance will not be maintained. Although the temptations will leave for a season, they do come back, and we must be prepared to resist. Yes, I was delivered from stealing, and I know that God did it, but what exactly is deliverance?

Deliverance means to be freed of the demonic forces that are assigned to kill our spirits, steal our joy, and ultimately destroy our lives. Deliverance can be as mild as reading the Word daily while God purges you of evil spirits to as serious as a deliverance team commanding demonic spirits to leave a person. Demons are enemies of the gifts and fruits of the Spirit. They try to keep the fruit from coming forth in the life of a person. They are spirit beings. They are enemies of God and man. Their objective in human beings is to tempt, deceive, accuse, condemn, defile, resist, oppose, control, steal, afflict, kill, and destroy. They enter through open doors, but they have to be given an opportunity to enter, an invitation, if you will. Otherwise, they cannot just come and go in and out of a person's life as they please. Whenever you commit a sin, you open a door. That is the invitation.

There is much controversy on the subject of demons, demonic forces, ungodly spirits, etc., but they are real and do exist whether we believe they do or not. And the sad reality is that many demons work directly with Christians. Many of these Christians are well dressed, respectable, and have the "appearance" of being refined and educated. While many profess Christian truths in order to appease their consciences, they live their lives in agreement with demonic forces, and the assigned demons grow and direct their actions very easily. It is critical, that we realize that the majority of demons influence Christians from the outside. They operate *around* them and not *in* them as with some non-Christians. Believers need only to stop agreeing with evil influences in order to get freed of them. The power of demons is rooted entirely in deception. Satan's power depends on the agreement of Christians with the ways of evil. Man is able to change his outward behavior for various self-centered and deceptive reasons, but only the spirit of God can change a man's heart. But although Satan may be able to counterfeit form, he can never counterfeit the fruit of the spirit. *You shall know them by their fruit* (Mathew 7:16) Deliverance must be maintained through prayer and fasting.

After overcoming temptations, I then realized that temptation is not a lasting condition. It is a passing phase, and once it is conquered, it ceases to be a temptation. As a student, ready to learn and understand knowledge and wisdom, I discovered that temptations come from inside a person, not circumstances surrounding a person. Temptations show us where we are sinful and ignorant. The source and cause of all temptation is the inward desire. Outside objects are really powerless to move a soul to be tempted. The outward object is just the element of the temptation, but the *desire* comes from *inside* of the one tempted. If the source and desire was in the object, then everyone would be tempted by the same things, but that is not the case. However, without temptations, a soul could not grow and become strong.

THE ARMOR

As I continued to fall in love with God, I realized that He is worthy of daily praise and worship, so I made a decision to develop a *good* habit of sacrificing my sleep and rising early to praise and worship Him. With this spiritual self-discipline, I began rising at 4:30 in the morning.   It was very hard,   but I forced myself to get up at the moment the alarm clock would sound. It eventually became second nature to me. There were days that I would forget to set the alarm, but would still be awakened by the Holy Spirit at exactly 4:30a.m. When it first happened, I thought it was merely a coincidence, but it happened too many times after that, so I knew it was God waking me up. God is not a respecter of persons, but He does give favor to those who praise and worship Him. As we draw closer and closer to Him, we no longer want just His gifts, but we want the Giver of the gifts. We no longer desire the blessings only, we want the Blesser.

Although prayer is very powerful, we must also keep ourselves spiritually covered. The precious shed blood of Jesus does cover us, but we must also put on the *"Armor of God."* While we do not see the armor, it is real in the spirit world, and it also affects the physical realm. When we clothe ourselves with the armor, we step out of the house fully equipped to quench all the fiery darts shot by spiritual enemies. A soldier would not go to war without his armor. We are in a spiritual war, and we must certainly not go out into this cruel and dangerous world without the proper gear. It is vital to our spiritual body that we put on the Armor of God. *Be strong in the Lord and in the power of His might. Put on the whole Armor of God, that you may be able to stand against the wiles of the devil. For we wrestle not against flesh and blood, but against principalities, against powers, against the rulers of the darkness of this world, against spiritual wickedness in high places. Wherefore take unto you the whole armor of God, that you may be able to withstand in the evil day, and having done all to stand. Stand therefore, having your loins girded about with truth, and having on the breastplate of righteousness,   and   your feet shod with the preparation of the gospel of peace; above all, taking the shield of faith wherewith you will be able to quench all the fiery darts of the wicked. And take the helmet of salvation, and the sword of the Spirit, which is the Word of God; praying always with all prayer and supplication in the Spirit, being watchful with all perseverance and supplication for all the saints...* (Ephesians 6:10-18). Keep yourself covered. Be wise as a serpent, but harmless as a dove.

IN THE THRONE ROOM

Being in the presence of God is a beautiful and glorious experience, but everything has a price. Spiritual necessities must be purchased. Money cannot buy them, but something must be given up before one can receive them.   I had to give up myself, my selfish desires, and my fleshly cravings for material things that were not mine nor rightfully mine to have. One may love their money and their fleshly possessions, but must give some of those things up or their desire and love for those things before they can receive the true peace and comfort of spirituality. Essentially, it is the desire for things that must be sacrificed. When you enter the throne room to be with the Lord, His Glory is reflected upon your countenance, and you feel the presence of God permeating all around you. It is an indescribable feeling, but one   that   leaves you   confident, strong, and free from fear. It is a wonderful feeling to be able to walk in His justification and glory all day with your head held high! He desires your praise and He inhabits the praises of His people (Psalm 22:3). He loves praises and He loves when we sacrifice the time to come be with Him. There is a song from Donald Lawrence and the Tri-City Singers that I love to listen to. It is called *In the Presence of a King.* Some of the lyrics are the following: *Do you know what it is? Can I tell you how it is? ...oh, to know how it feels, to be in the presence of a King... It's an honor and a privilege to be in the presence of a King... such an honor and a privilege to be in the presence of the King.* Oh yes, I know what it's like to be in the presence of the King. Do you? He will stop what He is doing to come and sit in the midst of your praise. He wants you to acknowledge Him. He wants you to tell Him how much you love Him, how much you admire and adore Him, how much you appreciate Him for who He is. Bless Him for this very moment. Thank Him right now for your health, your strength, your family, your friends, your job, your stable mind, and the ability to be able to read this book. Honor Him for what He is getting ready to do in your life. Most importantly, thank Him for His son Jesus, your Lord, Savior, and Redeemer. Our lips and hearts must praise Him. He is worthy and although He is no respecter of persons, He does give favor to those who praise and worship Him in Spirit and in truth, regardless of who they are. God is both the giver and the gift. We should thank God the giver, for God the gift. There is nothing like having an intimate relationship with Him. Our spirit must learn to listen to what He is saying. He speaks to your needs and gives you guidance so that His will can be manifested in your life. This is only learned by spending time with Him. Mere knowledge about Him is not the same as a personal relationship with Him. For without Jesus, you would have no access to God. Walk in Wisdom. Develop good habits and practice them daily.

~~ LESSONS LEARNED ~~

1. When you truly desire to serve the Lord, He will deliver you from every stronghold that would keep you bound.

2. The "Armor of God" protects from the spiritual bullets that are shot at men and women of God. No longer will I go into battle without putting on the whole *Armor of God* daily.

3. Character is not permanent. It is one of the most changeable things in nature. By a conscience act of the will, it is being constantly modified and reformed for the better by the pressure of circumstances.

~~REFLECTION QUESTIONS~~

1. What is the stronghold in your life that you need God to deliver you from? How do you plan on obtaining your freedom from it?

2. How do you handle temptations when they come your way? Do you resist, or do you give in? Are you passing the tests of temptation?

3. Do you put on the Armor of God during your prayer time before you leave the house? Are you walking into battle with your gear on?

*C*hapter
2

A Spirit of Excellence
The Gift of Teaching

The person who is constantly hesitating between
which of two things he or she will do, will do
neither. If you waver from plan to plan, goal to goal, and
constantly bend back and forth in the wind like a lily, you will
never accomplish anything great or useful. It is those who
concentrate on but one thing at a time who advance in this
world.

Not many things scattered, but one thing focused on is the
demand of our world. If you scatter your efforts, you will not
succeed. Decide on your goals and keep them forever in your
thoughts until they have been effectively achieved.

The great difference between those who succeed and those who
fail does not consist in the "amount" of work done by each, but
the amount of "quality" work. Never again should you lay only
your hands on your work when you can give your entire being.
Whatever you begin to do, you must do, as if nothing else in the
world is of greater importance. Concentration and perseverance
built the great pyramids.

One of the great joys of this life comes from doing everything you attempt to do to the best of your ability. There is a special sense of satisfaction; a pride in reviewing such a work, a work which is accurate, full, exact, and complete in all its parts, which a mediocre person who leaves his or her work in a half-finished condition, can never know.

The smallest task well done becomes a miracle of achievement. Accomplishment of whatever kind is the crown of effort, the diadem of thought. You cannot pursue a worthy goal steadily and persistently, with all the powers of your mind, and yet fail. Work with excellence each task performed.

A SPIRIT OF EXCELLENCE

An excellent spirit clearly means working with pride, pleasure, and significance in all one does. When I think of the spirit of excellence, I think of the Prophet Daniel, who had a flawless character. There is nothing written in the scriptures about Daniel that would cause one to taint his image. Daniel always stood for God and always endured every test with wisdom and integrity. Daniel's spirit was impeccable in terms of being holy and committed to his God. It is written that Daniel was preferred above all the presidents and princesses, because an "excellent spirit" was found in him (Daniel 6:3).

In the book of Daniel, the Jews were taken into captivity because they were continuously rebellious and refused to turn from their wicked ways, even after they had been given multiple warnings. They had practiced idolatry, which was an abomination, and because of this, God allowed various nations to take over their government and rule over them. Daniel was about 13 years old when he was forced to go into the Babylonian captivity. While there, he was made to learn a new language and respond to a new name given to him. They also wanted to change his diet and his religion. He was Hebrew, and it was against Hebrew religion to eat certain food and meat. But King Nebuchadnezzar wanted Daniel to abandon his dietary laws and conform to the Babylonian lifestyle, their culture, their religion, etc. The psychology behind changing a name is to change a person's identity so that they would forget everything about their past. Therefore, the king gave Daniel the new name of Belteshaz'zar. He offered Daniel the best of his meat and the best of his wine, and basically told him to, "*Eat my meat, drink my wine, and be a part of my kingdom.*" What the king was really saying was, "*Forget about your past and what you are use to and embrace your new life, a good life.*" This not only interfered with Daniel's religion but also his relationship with his God. However, this 13-year-old young man possessed something inside of him that would not allow him to accept what the king offered, nor would he eat the king's food. *Daniel purposed in his heart that he would not defile himself with the portion of the king's meat, nor with the wine which he drank* (Daniel 1:18). He said "*no*" to the king because of the spirit of God that was inside of him. At such a young age, this child was filled with the Word of God and clung to it with his heart. Daniel had an excellent spirit!

A GOOD NAME

Daniel had developed a reputation for being a good and credible young man. He had a gift of interpreting dreams and all of his interpretations came to pass (... *and Daniel had understanding in all visions and dreams.* 1:17).But it was not only his spiritual gifts that made him favored. It was the way he carried himself. There was something characteristic about Daniel that caught the eyes of the leadership. When he spoke, he answered with counsel and wisdom (*Daniel 2:14*). He was a diligent young man, who was given to precision. He was described as ...*having no blemish, but well favored and skillful in all wisdom, and cunning in knowledge, and understanding science and such as had ability in them to stand in the king's palace...* (*Daniel 1:4*). Daniel was dependable to the point that he was elevated in various heathen kingdoms to be a leader over many. Can you imagine a slave becoming a leader? It was because of his excellent spirit.

There is something about the spirit of a person that tells you where that person stands spiritually, emotionally and intellectually. There is something about a person's attitude that tells you whether or not you can trust him or her and whether he or she is a person of worth or not. Today we value people by their personality, charisma, and social skills, and are disappointed later on because we failed to realize that it is "character" that makes that person worthy more than charisma and social skills. Personality and charisma may open doors but character and integrity will keep them open.

THE "A" WORD

Accountability seems to be a nasty word today. People do not want to be held accountable when they know their work is sloppy. If both you and I are mediocre in our performance, then that's fine because no one stands out, but when I perform with mediocrity and you perform with excellence, that makes both of us stand out, one for good and one for bad. It also puts pressure on me to work harder. The "excellent" pays attention to all his duties and does everything wisely, thoughtfully, and efficiently. Unfortunately, mediocrity seems to be the standard for today's time, yet everyone wants a great employee evaluation. God wants and deserves the best in everything we do, whether it is washing the dishes, cleaning the house, making the bed, taking out the trash, sweeping the floor, or entertaining a guest. Whatever you do, do it as unto the Lord. When you give of yourself to your local church family or community, but neglect to ensure that your own household has been taken care of, you are not walking in a spirit of excellence. When you feed the hungry, but have not fed your own children, you are not walking in a spirit of excellence. When you teach Sunday School, but have not taught your own children the Word of God, you are not walking in a spirit of excellence. When your appearance is flawless, but your own children are unkempt, you are not walking in a spirit of excellence. One who has a spirit of excellence does *everything* to the best of their ability whether others are watching or not, and there is One above who is *always* watching. Those who are elevated naturally and spiritually are those with a track record of accomplishment.

Daniel had to be accountable to heathen kings, but God still gave him favor because of his excellent spirit. It is written in the scriptures that the king was so impressed with Daniel's spirit that he ... *made him a great man and gave him many great gifts, and made him ruler over the whole providence of Babylon* (Daniel 2:48). However, people were jealous and envious of Daniel because of it, and they plotted against him. And so it is today. People will plot against, talk bad about, and scrutinize everything you do when you have an excellent spirit. There is a price to be paid for being outstanding. Not everyone is going to like you when you walk in a spirit of excellence. Whenever you

19

want things done accurately and efficiently, people begin to complain about you. Whenever you strive to do your best, people become suspicious and begin to watch you closely. However, God will keep you covered and protect you on every side. People may plot and plan against you, but it is very dangerous to plot against a praying saint! One cannot wickedly plot against a child of God without consequences. A praying saint has angels with them everywhere they go. They have angels on the right side and angels on the left side, and angels in the front and back of them. They have goodness and mercy that follow them all the days of their life. They are well protected. They may not seem like much or look like much in the natural, but a praying child of God is a dangerous person to plot against! Continue walking in the spirit of excellence. Let what happened to the men who plotted against Daniel be a lesson to those who would think to plot against you: *And the king commanded, and they brought those men which had accused Daniel, and they cast them into the den of lions, them, their children, and their wives: and the lions had the mastery of them, and brake all their bones in pieces or ever they came at the bottom of the den* (Daniel 6:24). We always reap what we sow.

THE COST OF DISCIPLINE

Discipline goes hand in hand with having a spirit of excellence. Daniel prayed in the morning, in the afternoon, and in the evening. As busy as he was, he found the time to meet God. In order to have an excellent spirit, you must have a lifestyle of prayer. Only God can give you an excellent spirit and it comes by spending time with Him. Daniel had a busy schedule, yet he was disciplined. We are too busy working, going to school, doing so many things that we do not have designated time for God. We sometimes hang out so late that we can't even get up in the morning to pray. Daniel found time to pray not just once, not just twice, but three times a day. He met God in the morning, at noon, and at night. Meeting God should be a daily event. You may not be able to keep the same time every day, but you must be consistent. The secret in Daniel's excellent spirit was consistency. Do you desire to walk in the spirit of excellence? Then walk with God consistently and you will walk in an excellent spirit.

THE HIGH SCHOOL CHALLENGE

I can recall many instances where I performed mediocre to below what I had the potential to do. High school is what stands out the most. Without much effort, I was always at the top of my class in elementary school. The potential to excel above normal has always been in me, but I did not demonstrate it during middle nor high school. I goofed off and made bad grades from junior high on through high school. I just did not care. Socializing and modeling my clothes were my primary reasons for going to school. My grades were so low that I almost did not graduate. In fact, most people had already counted me as a lost case. No-one expected that I would graduate from high school or amount to anything worthy. Had it not been for my mother, I probably never would have finished. She stepped in and insisted that I take night classes and do whatever else I needed to do in order to graduate high school on time.

When it was time for graduation, I still needed one half of a credit. My mother went out to the school and talked to the principal about the situation. She managed to convince him to allow me to participate in the ceremony and she assured him that

I would take the last class needed. God touched his heart, and he said that if I came in for one day to help out in the main office the following Monday after graduation, he would give me my diploma, and I would not have to take that half-credit course. He warned me that I'd better show up and be on time. My mother thought that was a miracle. That was all I needed to do to receive my high school diploma.

I walked across that stage, shook my principal's hand with pride, and enjoyed the sense of accomplishment and bliss that my friends and I were experiencing. Monday came and the alarm clock sounded. I turned it off and rolled back over in my bed. My mother came in my room and snatched the covers off me. She told me that I'd better get dressed and get out to that school to work in that office so that I could get my high school diploma. Needless-to-say, I worked in the school's office and received my high school diploma.

Things never should have happened that way. I should have graduated with honors at the top of my class. I did not take my education seriously at the time, and I almost paid dearly for it. After graduation, I had no plans of going to college. The thought did not even cross my mind. After high school, I managed to get a job making seven dollars an hour, which was an excellent salary at the time. I thought I had it made earning that kind of money when the minimum wage was $3.35 an hour. I was still living with my mother, going to work and hanging out with my friends (the wrong crowd). My acquaintances, at the time were uneducated, had many children, lived in low-income housing, and frequented the clubs every week. These were the same people with whom I shoplifted.

THE DORM ROOM

The situation at home was not good between my mom and me. We constantly argued and all I wanted to do was move out of her house. I just could not stand her. Every woman needs her own house when she gets to be a certain age. I was then 19 years old, a woman, and needed my own place and my own space since I did not want to mind nor obey my mother's rules. I will never forget the day I had just arrived home from work when the phone rang. The man on the other end said, "*Hello this is Mr. Butler calling to let Michelle know that her dorm room at the college is ready.*" I said, "*There is no Michelle at this number, but can you tell me a little bit more about the dorm room?*" The man began explaining how I could move into the college dorm. I continued to ask questions about this dorm room and he, perceiving that my only interest was in the dorm room, proceeded to say, "*You can't just live in the dorm. You have to enroll in classes as a college student.*" I had not thought about that. I just wanted to get out of my mother's house and living in the dorm seemed just the right thing for me. I scheduled an appointment to meet him, registered for classes, and moved in the dorm the next day.

REALITY SINKS IN

My classes were all in the evening since I worked during the day. I continued my daily routine of going to work and attending school in the evening until one day... I had an awakening. Out of nowhere, it hit me that I was actually a real college student. I was a college junior, making straight As and Bs and was on the path to becoming a teacher! Initially, when I registered for classes, I never chose any major. I simply went to an advisor who I was directed to see, and he chose my classes for me every semester. He was in the school of education, so naturally, all my classes were education courses.

I walked in a spirit of excellence while in college. I was a good student. I attended all my classes on time, was never absent, studied hard and made good grades. Yet, I never really gave any thought to what I was doing. God was navigating the circumstances of my life. My destiny was unfolding right in front of me, and I was oblivious to what was happening until that day when I was awakened. From that moment on, I consciously took control of my life. I began to reflect on how I had gotten to that point. The more I reflected, the more astounded I was at how everything in my life was falling into place. I was humbled and grateful for what God had done for me. I had been reading the bible during my leisure time and also going to church on Sundays. I did not steal anymore, did not use profanity anymore, and did not hang with the same people anymore. Praise God! I graduated Cum Laude from Florida Memorial University in the spring of 1994. I had earned a college degree!

Becoming a teacher was very exciting for me and I eagerly anticipated the undertaking. However, getting hired did not come without obstacles. Since I had managed to get myself arrested in my adolescent years, I had to give an account of what happened for each arrest, explain why I did it, and convince a panel of people at the Office of Professional Standards why they should hire me. God, in His grace and mercy saw to it that I was hired.

THE ALTERNATIVE STUDENTS

I couldn't wait to bring my creative teaching styles into the classroom. I felt that there were too many children in this world who were below grade level and way too many who could not read or write. I had purposed in my heart to be the best teacher that I could be. I was determined that my students would learn and would leave my tutelage with a wealth of knowledge. I had a successful first year teaching third graders, and I could really see that teaching was one of my God-given gifts. My second year however, was a bit more challenging. Upon completion of my first year, the principal approached me about teaching the 4th grade Alternative Education (AE) class for the next school year. This class consisted of students who displayed severe behavioral and emotional problems although they had not been professionally diagnosed as having such problems. I had seen those students around the school and it was obvious that they were in a "special" class. I had seen their antics and display of disciplinary problems, so I knew that it would take a strong teacher to educate those types of students. They were very intimidating. I was very hesitant to accept the position at first, so she asked me to think about it. She stated that she felt I would do an excellent job with those students, and that she saw the ability in me. There was also a $1,200 stipend that came with teaching in the program. I knew that the position had to be challenging if the school district was willing to give extra money for teaching the class. Nevertheless, I accepted the position.

My first week with the students was a huge test. They walked in my classroom with attitudes out of this world, throwing temper tantrums, knocking over desks and chairs, using profanity, yelling and screaming, refusing to sit down, refusing to do any class work, etc. I knew that I could not show any sign of intimidation, but I had to do something. So I did some of the same things they did. When they knocked over a desk, I knocked over one. When they threw a chair, I threw one, and so on. I told them that there could not be more than one crazy person in the class at a time, and that the crazy one was me. They began to realize that I was just as crazy as they wanted me to think they were. I stood my ground, did not waver, laid down the rules, was consistent in what I said, set the tone in the classroom, and it was smooth sailing after that.

I put my entire being into getting to know each and every one of my students personally, and I succeeded. I learned that many of them had been psychologically wounded and emotionally scared. However, I taught them with excellence. There were students in my class who had been abused, neglected, some raped. Many of them were living with grandparents because their parents were incarcerated or on drugs. Some lived with foster parents and some were in shelters. Others were just plain defiant and needed firm discipline. That's when I learned that we must get to the root cause of the misbehavior in children. They are not as adults, in that they can express themselves effectively and tell us what is wrong with them. They don't know how to say, *"I'm hurting because my mother is on drugs, and she lives in the street. I miss my mother, and I think about her at night when I'm in my bed. I just want my mom to come home."* When children are hurting, most often they misbehave as an escape mechanism. They need to understand that no matter what outer behavior they find themselves presenting, there is still goodness inside of them. When we cannot see beyond the behavior, we begin to dislike and sometimes mistreat the children. All too often, we neglect to separate the behavior from the person. It is imperative that we begin to articulate to children that although we reject their behavior at times, we still accept them and love them.

Working with those young children helped me to realize that there is a great need to reach out to underprivileged youth. Unfortunately, many in disenfranchised communities are often compromised in the school system academically, financially, and also psychologically. Unfortunately, the unmet needs of our children impact their ability to be effective in their learning. Children need to be able to talk about their fears, hurts, and pains. They need an outlet. They need the same things adults need, to feel loved, to be able to give love, to feel safe and secure, accepted, appreciated, and respected.

I became so close to my students that I prayed for each one of them individually. They made tremendous progress in their attitudes, their outlook on life, their respect for others and themselves, and their academic performance. When their attitudes changed for the better and they allowed light to shine in their hearts, their academics improved. Every morning after the Pledge of Allegiance, I would have a student recite a thought for the day in front of the class to start off the day positively. They would stand up and say something like: *"The thought for the day is: Don't look for miracles because you are a miracle."* There were positive affirmations all around my classroom. We would then have a discussion regarding what the statement meant to them, and how they were going to apply it into their lives.

My students were overprotective of me and there was a strong bond between all of us. They trusted me, and I was able to trust them. When it was time for the school year to end, I cried because I did not want to see them go. They had blossomed. They had flourished. They had developed a sense of pride. They had just completed the fourth grade. I was adamant in making a positive change in those students, and I did. I worked with excellence towards the task at hand. I taught alternative education students every year thereafter, and I still kept the same attitude about making a difference in the lives of those challenging students who are only crying out for love and attention. I make sure I give it to them too.

~~ LESSONS LEARNED ~~

1. Displaying love towards God's children will bring out the best inside of them and cause their gifts to manifest into the earth realm.

2. When we focus on walking in righteousness, reading the Word and praying, God will navigate our lives so that our feet will walk on the path that He has pre-destined for us.

3. If you look at children the way they are in the natural, they only become worse, but when you see the good that God has placed inside of them, they become what they should be.

~~ REFLECTION QUESTIONS ~~

1. Do you strive for excellence in what you do, or are you a mediocre person who does only enough to get by?

2. Is there potential inside of you that you are not allowing to manifest into your life?

3. Are you disciplined enough to designate a specific prayer time each day to spend with God?

*C*hapter

3

Find the Good in Every Situation
Loving the Unlovable

ook at all things with love and become renewed.

Speak with love. Behave with love. React to the actions of others with love. Face each day and every person you meet with love, and love yourself.

Love the sun because it warms you; Love the rain because it cleanses your spirit.
Love the light because it shows you the way; Love the darkness because it shows you the stars.
Welcome happiness because it enlarges your heart; Endure sadness because it opens your soul.
Acknowledge rewards because they are your due; Welcome obstacles because they are your challenge.

Find the good in every situation!

How should you speak? Extol your enemies and they will become friends; Encourage your friends and they will become brothers and sisters. Always dig for reasons to applaud; never look for excuses to gossip. When you are tempted to criticize, bite your tongue; when you are moved to praise, shout on the roof!
Find the good in every situation!

HOW WE THINK IS HOW WE ACT

Has anyone ever said to you, *"I see you woke up on the wrong side of the bed this morning?"* What exactly do they mean when they say that? They mean that your disposition and attitude seems to be negative that day. The energy that you are releasing is negative and you may be walking with a bad vibration. Some people refer to this as bad karma. We probably are exhibiting moody or contentious behaviors. Because of our negative mood, folks tend to stay away from us, not wanting to be around the negativity that we are giving off. As true men and women of God, we must walk in stability, not allowing our thoughts and feelings to control our behaviors. Our attitudes must be positive regardless of what we may be thinking, feeling, or what circumstances we may be facing. Attitudes parallel with what is in the mind, and attitudes do reflect thinking. We must begin to think about what we are thinking about and force our attitude and behavior to be positive. Our thoughts are revealed in how we act and how we act, determines how others act towards us. People do read attitudes through body language, voice tones, and inflections. We must realize the impact that a positive attitude has on every interpersonal relationship in our lives. I once heard the Reverend Jackie McCullough, one of my favorite Christian Ministers recite a quote that her mother use to say: *"Even if you don't have money, if you have a positive attitude and good manners, that can take you all over the world."* That quote resonated in my mind, because I thought that it was so simple and yet so true. When our attitude is right, our abilities reach a maximum of effectiveness and good results will follow. Winston Churchill said, *"Attitude is a little thing that makes a big difference."* The ability to maintain a positive attitude, especially in the midst of challenges, is an asset that can never be measured. This asset is used for making meaning out of our environment, circumstances, relationships, conversations, and problems that are experienced in life. Maintaining a positive attitude is about choices in emotional responses. People with this ability choose their focus instead of allowing circumstances to dictate their focus. They tend to remain in a rational state of mind, and make the most of whatever life offers them. These individuals know how to seize the day and create good memories by projecting a positive future. They solve problems as quickly as possible. They often do more, go further, and experience more enjoyable, fulfilling and satisfying lives.

Yes, it is true that we do not always wake up bright-eyed and bushy tailed, but we can *force* ourselves into having good days regardless of how we may feel when we wake up in the morning or how terrible the day has started off to be. We cannot directly choose what our days will entail, but we can choose our thoughts and indirectly, yet surely, shape our circumstances. Walking in a negative vibration will open doors to all sorts of stressful situations to be drawn to us, which work against us. When others see constant patterns of negative dispositions and different personalities in us, derogatory opinions are formed and this creates adverse situations in our lives. When there is constant conflict, discord, and confusion in a person's life, that is an indication that there is conflict, discord and confusion inside of that person. Whatever is experienced on the outside is only a tangible manifestation of what already exists on the inside. As the within, so the without. We must let the light that God has placed in us shine daily. We cannot hide it on bad days, and let it shine on good days. Doing this is indicative of instability and double-mindedness, and according to the bible in James 1:8, *"a double-minded man is unstable in all his ways"*.

One who dwells day by day in thoughts of peace towards every person, will bring a wealth of peace to themselves. What

31

you say of another will be said of you, and what you are wishing for another, you are wishing for yourself. Life is a mirror, and as we look with admiration, those God-given characteristics in others, we are actually looking at what God has placed inside of us. We find ourselves reflected in others.

THE POWER OF LOVE

Genuine love is selfless and free from fear. Its joy is in the joy of giving. Love is the strongest force in the universe. It is God in manifestation. It is our greatest weapon, piercing the hard hearts of many. Love is also our shield to cast off arrows of hatred and spears of anger. When adversity and discouragement beat against our shield, they will eventually become the softest of rains. If you do everything out of love you will always triumph. Love is the source of courage and it will prevail in the end. There is perfect peace, courage, and power in love. If we are really committed to walking in love, speaking in love, and encountering others with love, then when facing difficult people, the spirit of love will break down their hard exteriors and penetrate to the goodness inside them, causing them to love in return. It may not happen immediately, but a persistent drop in the same spot, will cause the strongest cement to soften. If you find yourself in a situation wherein you must interact with a difficult person and it really bothers you, try this: In your quiet time alone, address the spirit of that person in prayer and say to their spirit, *"I love you."* Though spoken in silent prayer, these three words will open the heart of the individual, and you will eventually win him or her over with your newfound love and perception of him or her. You can never receive what you have never given. Give a perfect love, and you will receive a perfect love.

Many of us try to change other people. To live in peace with others, we do not need to change them. We need to change ourselves. Others will change as we change our thoughts and feelings about them. Regardless of what they have done, you absolutely must find the strength to forgive and release them, not for them but for you and for the sake of your sanity and your health. Contrary to what the enemy speaks to your mind, it does not take much to forgive and release. In fact, it takes more strength, effort, and energy to hold grudges, harbor bitterness, hatred, and unforgiveness. Do not think that courage lies only in physical boldness. The greatest courage is the courage to be higher than your anger and to forgive a person who has offended or hurt you.

THE RESULT OF KINDNESS

It does not take much effort to smile and be kind. You never know just how much your kind words or deeds will impact someone's life who has been feeling down, depressed, hopeless, or distressed. Your smile alone may brighten their day and give them hope for a better tomorrow. On the contrary, your mean attitude or ugly look may push a person over the edge. You do not want that on your conscience. Every chance we have to be kind and show mercy and grace, is a great opportunity for us to receive more mercy and more grace from the Lord. We must begin knowing one another after the spirit and seeing each other as God sees us. When we start to see the good in that which seems worthless, and begin speaking to it and drawing it out in one another, we will become the men and women who God has created us to be. Let us stop crucifying Christ again when He comes in even the least of His children, but let us start recognizing Him, honoring Him, and calling Him forth in one other. Find the good in everyone and every situation!

The words in this book or any book may be easy to read but hard to apply. It is also easy for me to write these words, but can be very challenging to apply to my own life. I am however, speaking from experience. I am still struggling with finding the good in everyone and every situation, especially when I cross paths with those who have hurt me, lied on me, used me, betrayed me, or hated me. But the more deliberate I am in trying to look at them with love, the less harder it becomes, until it is not so hard at all.

THE PRINCIPAL

In all my years of living, I have worked with many types of people with varying personalities, but there is one person who really stands out. She was the principal at the first school where I began to teach. I had completed my internship at her school and during the internship, she approached me and told me that she had been watching me and was very impressed with what she saw. She stated that my teaching skills were impeccable and she thought the way that I interacted with the students was very positive. She hired me fresh out of college.

I enjoyed working with the teachers, but it did not take me long to see that the principal was needless-to-say, a very disturbed woman. She seemed to gain a distorted sense of power by embarrassing, mistreating, and demeaning people. She was a liar and her unethical leadership practices, lack of decorum, and overall sadistic behaviors had caused a very large portion of the teachers and staff members to have very little respect for her. Ironically, she professed to be a devout Christian Minister. There were others however who walked in peace and true Godliness on the job, but strangely, she did not gravitate to those individuals. In fact, it seemed as though she tried to avoid them. Just as Cain could not tolerate Abel, those who seek to stand by their own

34

righteousness find the presence of those who stand by faith in Jesus, intolerable. The self-righteousness of those seeking to be justified by their own works is very shaky and deep inside they know it; because of this, they are easily threatened by anyone who would challenge their delusion. I had a wonderful first year of teaching and received many compliments from veteran teachers at the close of the school year. I loved teaching children, and I knew that teaching was my gift.

As time passed, I continued to see the unscrupulous behaviors displayed by the principal. She was very unprofessional and had a proclivity for publicly humiliating teachers. In one particular staff meeting, she told a teacher that she dressed like a hobo. The teacher was mortified. Her face turned red and her entire countenance changed. When I spoke with her the next day, she told me that she had cried all the way home. This principal would harass teachers for no apparent reason and try to force them to socialize only with certain individuals. She had several harassment complaints filed against her, but was never held accountable because her uncle was a very high executive within the school system and protected her. Many were afraid to file complaints because of who her uncle was, so she got away with many improprieties as the principal of that school.

IT'S MY TURN

She was very kind to me when I first started working there, but I began to dislike the way she treated others. It bothered me to see her mistreat and demean adults in the presence of other adults. She also disrespected teachers in the presence of their students. She began to perceive how I felt about her and the mistreatment towards me began. I was one of two union stewards, and when I would speak in faculty meetings, the teachers would be very attentive to the information given and would clap when I was finished because they appreciated the valuable information being given to them. I have learned that people appreciate valuable information that is beneficial to them. The principal told them that there was no need to clap for me, as they were not being entertained, but only receiving information. She approached the other union steward and told him that she did not want me giving the union updates anymore. Why did she not want me to speak? Was it because the teachers listened too attentively to the information that I was conveying? When he told me what she said, I told him that I had no problem with him disseminating the information to the teachers, but if he did not attend the union meetings as I had been, then how was he going to convey information that he had no knowledge of? When he told me that I needed to tell him the information and he would give it, I immediately realized what was happening. I told him that made no sense and to tell the principal that no one was going to stop me from talking. It was my job as a union steward to ensure that teachers receive information to which they were entitled. Furthermore, I told him that when he went to the Union Meetings and received the information himself, he then could disseminate it to the teachers. Until then, I would not neglect to give teachers first-hand information, simply because the principal had insecurity issues.

     This woman, a minister of the gospel caused those who were not saved to remain unsaved, substantiating their views of Christian hypocrites. The reason why people who knew her were not interested in her god is because she did not have enough of the presence of God in her life. The main reason why people do not turn their lives over to God based on what we say, is because they may be seeing too little of God in our lives, and too much of flesh. We absolutely have to practice walking upright and loving one other because souls are at stake. Our behavior does not only affect us. It affects many others - having a domino affect on people we don't even know. Those who truly know their God, are the most confident, peaceful, and humble people on earth. What does it profit a person to be able to profoundly discourse the Word of God, if he or she is void of humility and thereby displeasing to the Lord? The fruit of corruption that manifested in this woman's everyday walk was evident in her life and everyone could see it. *A corrupt tree cannot bring forth good fruit; neither can a good tree bring forth corrupt fruit* (Mathew 7:8). Fear, intimidation, strong controlling forces operated through her and made it difficult for anyone to speak out for what was right. Therefore, everyone continued to endure mistreatment and overlooked this woman's unethical practices and ineffective leadership skills. Sadly, teachers eventually became immune to the behaviors and accepted her antics as the norm. Although many teachers left, many also stayed, and I began to see and hear justifications made for her by those who had been teaching many, many years. It was amazing, yet sad to hear those who once stood up against what was wrong now justifying and compromising for what was wrong. I knew it was time for me to leave before my perceptions for what was right became distorted as well.

WHISPERING GRUMBLES

People constantly complained amongst each other about her, but did so secretly. They smiled, laughed, and continued to feed her insatiable ego while in her presence. Her lust for power was fueled by her insecurity. Her drive for control seemed to be a defense mechanism to protect her from rejection, but those who have truly surrendered to Christ will not be intimidated by others with knowledge or dismayed by rejection.

37

On the other hand, those who exercise authority with selfish motives are corrupt, regardless of their pretentious piety. It is important and very critical to realize that when we are truly surrendered to Christ, we should handle authority with the greatest care, knowing that we are His servants. No one is established authoritatively unless God allows it. God does share His authority with His people, and used in humility and submission, authority is a powerful tool. But when that power is used for self-exaltation, our leadership, effectiveness, and credibility is significantly diminished; and we do those under our leadership a great disservice. This principal was so self-exalted that she demanded children to stand up and greet her whenever she walked into a classroom, as though she were a Greek Goddess. To the unwise, authority is an opportunity for self-exaltation and self-promotion, but in Christ, the call to authority is a call for self-sacrifice. I could not conform to what I knew was wrong, and as a result, I was ostracized and mistreated.

The children were not allowed to speak to her while sitting down. They had to stand up, push in their chairs, and then greet her in unison. I absolutely detested that, but it was a school-wide rule, and I could not tell the children not to obey the principal. I prayed about it. We may not understand God's purpose in many things, but every authority that He permits to come into power is to bring about His purposes. I knew that. With that in mind, I tried to be respectful and humble when interacting with her, but it was very difficult to look past the natural exterior in order to understand the forces at work through her.

Everyone at the school saw the mistreatment towards me and others who she had targeted. People would hear negative comments that she would make about teachers and that put a bad taste in the mouths of many. Nonetheless, they still would not interact with or even look at us if she was in the vicinity to see it.

When she was not around however, people would shower us with kindness to alleviate their guilt. Others would tell me that they appreciated me for who I was and what I stood for. Some expressed that they felt that the mistreatment towards people was wrong, unnecessary, and downright wicked. Many offered words of encouragement. However, those same individuals would not openly speak with those who had been targeted by her for fear of reprisal. It was an unspoken rule that if anyone interacted with those whom she did not like, those individuals were automatically against her and would be subjected to the same mistreatment.

DIVISIONS IN THE WORKPLACE

This was a major test for me, but I continued to teach my students to the best of my ability and I gave them all I had on a daily basis. Regardless of how I was being treated by the principal, I never let it affect my performance in the classroom. I loved my students and I served them with commitment and diligence. I could not understand however, how one person could lead such a large group of individuals into conforming to what they knew was wrong. I had watched over the years how people who once spoke out for what was right had compromised what they stood for to appease this woman. They had been silenced and did not realize what had happened to them over the years. The spirits that controlled that woman were strong, and the desire of others to be on her good side was also strong. I observed how people would backstab their own friends by divulging their friend's personal business, all in the name of favor from this woman. We should never strive for man's approval. We need to be concerned about whether the King approves of us, not man. That school had become so divided that visitors could feel the polarity when they walked into the building. The tension in that school was so thick that it permeated the very atmosphere and the principal was the root cause for all of the dissension.

Although I loved teaching my Alternative Education students, I also loved the $1,200 stipend that came with it at the end of each school year. I looked forward to receiving that money because I usually did not work summer school and the money came in handy for the upcoming summer months. I will never forget the last 4th grade AE class that I taught. I loved them, but they were really a challenge. I had to run a really tight ship with that class. I was basically a drill sergeant for the entire first semester. This class had a total of three girls only and the rest were boys and they were rough. I really earned my salary with that class. When it came time for me to receive my stipend at the end of the school year, the money was not in my last paycheck, so I asked the principal about it. I was absolutely shocked at her response to me. She told me that I had not taught the AE class that year and that I had taught a regular 4th grade class. A regular 4th grade class? Everyone knew that I taught the AE class because they knew my students. At the beginning of each school year, letters were sent home informing parents of what the Alternative Education Program entailed and how the class was slightly different from a standard class. The principal herself had sent one of the clerical personnel to me at the beginning of the school year to make sure that I had received each letter back signed by the parents. These letters were kept in the main office. I had received a letter back from each student and I filed them into each cumulative folder myself. When I reminded her about this, she told me that I should not have sent those letters home, although she was the one who gave me the letters. They were pre-written and she gave them to me at the beginning of the school year and told me to make sure that I sent them home and received each one back.

When I asked her why I wasn't told that I was not teaching the class anymore (on paper), she told me that she and I had had a conversation about it, at which time she told me that I would no longer be teaching the class and therefore would not be getting a stipend at the end of the year. How in the world could I have not remembered such a conversation? The conversation never took place and she knew it. I asked her what my response was when she told me this, and she said that she did not remember. I was so angry that I blatantly said to her, *"You are a liar!"* and I walked off. I was so infuriated and shocked that an administrator would stand in the face of an employee and lie about something as significant as that. This was my livelihood that she played with just as she had done so many times before with other people. If she didn't have the money in her budget to pay me (and I don't know if that was the case) all she had to do was tell me from the beginning. I would have been disappointed, but would have gladly taught the children, because the gratification in seeing them turned around at the end of each school year was my reward; but she used and deceived me. I knew that it was time for me to go.

TIME FOR ACTION

Realizing that I must practice what I profess, I prayed for a change in me so that I could love this woman with an agape love regardless of her evil doings. It wasn't easy. After all, she was my superior, and I had to exercise respect and submission to her since she did have authority over me. It was really difficult because I wear my emotions on my face, and my facial expressions reveal how I feel about a person or situation without me having to say a word. Although I would try and smile at her when I spoke, I would deliberately send subliminal messages letting her know that I did not like nor respect her.

Other than the time that I called her a liar and walked off, I never again disrespected her. Trying to change for the better and being sincere about it was hard, but God gives us the strength to tear down those walls of pride in ourselves so that we can love others in spite of their ways. Loving the unlovable is not easy, but as we continue striving to be like God, He will transform us by the renewing of our mind so that we can love unconditionally. We must work out our own salvation with fear and trembling, but the working it out part is a process and a challenge. I made a decision to leave that school. It was difficult because I had been there for a few years. I knew that I eventually wanted to become an Assistant Principal, and in order to apply for the program that enabled aspiring administrators to be trained, their immediate supervisor needed to complete a recommendation form and checklist. I did not trust that her completion of the form would be honest or favorable. Therefore, after prayer and fasting, I humbly went to her and handed her a Transfer Form to sign. Initially, she seemed to be surprised but immediately collected herself and signed the form with a sinister, yet disappointing look on her face. She asked no questions and made no comments, at least not to me. Having already secured a position, I left the very next day. After I was gone, I decided to pursue getting the AE money that was rightfully owed to me. I called the Alternative Education Department and explained my situation. I was told that their records indicated that the principal had placed me in a regular 4th grade slot for that school year and unless I had proof that I taught the class, they could not pay me the stipend. I told the gentleman that I had sent letters home, which parents had signed at the beginning of the school year. He told me that if I could show him those signed letters, that would be proof enough. I needed to bring those letters to his office and I would be able to get paid. But there was only one problem. I no longer worked at the school, and therefore did not have access to the student records anymore. I called a friend who still worked there and asked her to copy the set for me. She called me back and told me that the letters had been taken out of the students' cumulative folders. After hearing that, I called and spoke with the clerk who had asked me for the signed forms at the beginning of the year. I distinctively remember making her a copy of the complete set before filing them in the students' cumulative folder. When I asked her what happened to the forms, she reluctantly told me that the principal made her shred them. The principal had gone to such measures just to ensure that I wouldn't get paid. I knew that I would not be getting the money then, so after that, I left the situation alone. I knew that God would take care of me.

THE LOSS OF A GOOD TEACHER

After I had been gone for a few days, I was called by ex-colleagues who told me that the principal was not happy about my leaving and was very upset by it. That was strange to me considering how indifferent she was when I handed her the transfer and how mean she had been to me. The truth is that I was extremely good at what I did because it was my gift, and when something is a God-given gift, you are good at it. I know that I had a positive impact in the lives of my students and the school. My commitment to excellence would not let me do it any other way and as a result, my dedication and loyalty to the children made the principal as well as the school shine. When standardized test scores were released, my students always ranked in the top three compared to the other classes on the grade level. One year, their writing scores were the second highest in the grade level. Some may ask why falling in the middle such a big deal? Because I taught the 4th grade Alternative Education Class. This class was comprised of at risk

43

"low-achieving" students with severe behavior problems. Needless-to-say, there was an overrepresentation of Black boys in the class compared to any other ethnic group or gender. These children had been given up on and basically counted out. Although they called it what they wanted, the class was really a dumping ground for Black boys with behavior problems. But those are the students I wanted. They called them trash, but when I was finished with them, they became treasures. The expectation was that their test scores would be at the bottom of the barrel, but that would not be the case so long as they were in my class. Children can and will learn once their behavior has changed for the better and when they have a good teacher willing to teach them. Learning will not take place until behavior is changed. The discipline gap mirrors the achievement gap. Discipline is love and in my class, they were loved much. I was later told by the principal's secretary that the principal secretly admired my strengths and intellect, but that her pride would never allow her to tell me. She revealed that the principal constantly bragged about what a great teacher I was and how she wished she had a memory like mine. She said that the principal had a high level of respect for me. Wow, is that how you treat someone you respect? I was confused and did not understand, but I did not spend a lot of time pondering on it. I had my future to look forward to at the new school.

    After leaving that school, I never spoke negatively about her and although I would hear others say derogatory things about her, I never commented. I felt that speaking negatively about another person, particularly a former boss, diminished that person, so I refused to diminish myself. I remembered a quote that I read from Benjamin Franklin when he was asked about his gift for positively interacting with people. He said, "*I will speak ill of no man... and speak all the good I know of everybody.*"

I left that negative experience behind me, and I looked with optimism to the future that I knew had many blessings waiting for me. I needed that experience to recognize what ineffective leadership looked like and the effect that it had on others. God was preparing me for effective leadership, and I needed to know the difference. Finding the good in everyone and every situation will also strengthen the spirit of discernment within one and open the spiritual ear to hear the voice of God clearly.

I thank God for the experience that I had at that school. Had I not worked there, I may not have had the opportunity to work with AE children, bring out their potential, and help to raise their self-esteem and respect for themselves and others. I also thank the principal for seeing the ability inside me and helping me to be successful in that position. I thank her for hiring me and teaching me by example that ineffective leadership can have a detrimental effect on staff morale. No man is your friend. No man is your enemy. Every man is your teacher. She taught me well and yes, I love her for it.

THE HOTDOG MAN

Speaking of love, I also recall a time when I was on my way to an interview for an Executive Secretary's position. It was for a huge pharmaceutical manufacturing company, and the position for which I was applying was way out of my league. I was in my early twenties, in college, and had to find a good paying job because I had accumulated bills that my current job salary of $7.50 per hour was not covering. The position for which I was applying paid $8,000 more per year, and although it was out of my league, I knew that if given the opportunity, I could do it. My clerical and interpersonal skills were pretty good, and I had always had a knack for interviewing well. I had managed to secure myself an interview. On the day of the interview, I was about 30 minutes early, so I walked to the hotdog stand across the street. The vendor was a tall, slender man from the West Indies. Somehow he and I began talking. I discerned that he had a wounded spirit and was disheartened about something. He revealed that his wife had just left him the day before. She said that she was not happy in the marriage anymore. He was devastated and began to weep as he talked to me. His heart was broken, and the compassion that I felt for him caused my heart to hurt. I offered him words of encouragement and assured him that I would pray for him. I meant that I really would pray for him because all too often, we hear the trials and tests that others go through, and we are so quick to say, *"I will pray for you"* and we never do. I guess that statement is a natural response when we know there really is nothing else that we can do or say, but if we say we are going to pray for someone, we need to pray for them. After I told him that, I went to the interview.

The interview went very well, and I was told to come back for a second interview days later. When I arrived home that evening, I not only prayed for that man, but I went to warfare for his marriage. I prayed as though he was my own relative. I went into the spirit realm and pulled down every force of darkness that came against his marriage. I prayed for comfort and peace for him. Then I prayed that his wife would return to her husband with a change of heart. I honestly felt a breakthrough in the spirit as I was praying and an overwhelming sense of assurance fell on me. I was extremely excited and full of joy because I knew that God had moved.

WHAT A GREAT DAY!

Days later, I returned back for my second interview with the company. I went to the hotdog stand to see my friend and to buy another hotdog. His face lit up when he saw me. This day, he was not selling hotdogs alone. He was with his wife who had come back home the day after I met him. I knew in my heart that God had heard my prayers because I had prayed for him with love in my heart. I went on to my final interview. God blessed me with that new job, where I became the Administrative Secretary to the President/CEO of that company, and where I remained until I graduated college and began teaching. I received two blessings that day!

~~ LESSONS LEARNED ~~

1. Taking a stand for what you know is right, will strengthen the character within you. Even when the mistreatment is not directed toward you personally, it should not be tolerated when we see others targeted.

2. Although it may not be easy working with certain individuals, look for the good in the situation and evaluate what you think the reason is that you have crossed paths with them in that season.

3. God hears and answers our prayers quickly when we pray with total love and compassion for others.

~~ REFLECTION QUESTIONS~~

1. Is your personality stable, or does your moodiness show in your thoughts, feelings, behavior, and actions?

2. When encountering difficult people, do you look for the goodness in them, or are you quick to treat them according to their faults and behaviors?

3. When you tell people that you are going to pray for them, do you really go home and pray for them?

*C*hapter

4

Laugh Often
It's Better to Have Loved and Lost

*N*o *living creature can laugh except human beings. Only humans have this gift of laughter, and it is ours to use whenever we choose.*

When you smile, your digestion improves; When you chuckle, your burdens are lightened; When you laugh, your life is lengthened, for this is the great secret to long life, and now it is yours.

Can you laugh when confronted with person or deed, which offends you so as to bring forth your tears or makes you want to curse? Certainly! Four words you can train yourself to say until they become a habit so strong that immediately they appear in your mind whenever good humor threatens to depart from you. These words will carry you through every adversity and maintain your life in balance. These four words are: THIS TOO SHALL PASS.

For all worldly things shall indeed pass. When you are heavy with heartache, you shall console yourself with, "This too shall pass." When you are puffed up with success, you shall warn yourself with, "This too shall pass." When you are burdened with wealth, you must tell yourself, "This too shall pass." If all worldly things shall indeed pass, why should you be of concern for today?

And with laughter all things will be reduced to their proper sizes. Laugh at your failures and they will vanish into clouds of new dreams. Laugh at your successes and they will shrink to their proper sizes. Laugh at evil, and it will die untasted! Laugh at goodness, and it will thrive and abound!

Never should you allow yourself to become so important, so wise, so dignified, and so powerful, that you forget how to laugh at yourself. In this manner, you will remain as humble as a child, for only as a child are you given the ability to look up to others.

THE MYSTERY MAN

Many of us have heard the saying *"It's better to have loved and lost than never to have loved at all."* That may very well be true, and there is nothing like the "feeling" of being in love. In all my years of living, I have been in love twice. I thought that I was in love at other times, but looking back in retrospect, I was in love with the *idea* of being in love. A friend of mine once told me that unconditional love between a man and a woman does not exist. He said that unconditional love existed between parents and children only. Love between men and women was, in his opinion conditional. As I pondered on his reasoning, I began to realize that he was right. We think that we are in love with people because of how they treat us and how they make us feel, but as soon as they begin to mistreat us or step out of the boundaries that we have created for them, we don't love them anymore. Our love is indeed conditional. Let me introduce you to Robert. I had been seeing him in services, and I noticed how faithful he was in coming to church. He was always quiet and seemed to be very attentive to the Word of God as it would go forth. He always sat alone and would leave immediately following church services. I really liked how he carried himself and for months, I admired him from afar. I didn't even know his name.

One Tuesday evening following Bible Study, I arrived to the parking lot to find a note under the windshield of my Eclipse. The note read: *"Hi, my name is Robert. I think you are gorgeous. I have seen you in church many times and I admire the way you praise the Lord. If it's not too late, please give me a call tomorrow,* and he left his number. I was flattered to get a note, but I did not know who this secret admirer was, so I did not call, at least not right away. I wondered for a couple of days who could have left the note. In the back of my mind, I wished it was the person who I had been secretly admiring for so long, but I knew that was a long shot. I did not want to call the number for fear that it would be someone that I would be completely unattracted to, so I held off on calling. Our church was so big that it could have been anyone. After all, New Birth Baptist Church had over 7,000 members at that time.

MYSTERY MAN REVEALED

About four days later, I called and had a conversation with my secret admirer. He told me that he would reveal himself to me the next Tuesday night at Bible Study. He explained that he had to leave church early the night he left the note on my car because he had to be to work at 4:00a.m., and needed to get some rest. Otherwise, he would have approached me personally, he stated. He was a supervisor at United Parcel Service. We had interesting conversations, and he seemed very intelligent, but I still was hesitant about talking too much without seeing him first. Bible Study finally came and all throughout the service I thought about the revelation that I was to get that night. I could not concentrate on the Word that evening because my mind kept wandering off.

When service was over and the congregation was walking out, I wondered if he had seen me because I was almost out the door, but just before I stepped out completely, a man approached me and said, *"Hi Mia, I'm Robert. I am the one who put the note on your car."* It was him, the guy that I had admired for so long! I was so excited, but of course I did not show it. I was as smooth as silk. I remember thinking, *"Thank You Jesus!"* Maybe I had sent him some sort of subliminal messages that led him to me. That was not the first time that a man I had admired from afar had come to me. We talked in the parking lot for a while, and I gave him my phone number. After dating for a couple of weeks, we decided to become exclusive, and he insisted that we begin going to church together. He possessed many of the characteristics that I was attracted to and desired in a man. He was handsome, had a great job, was educated, a complete gentleman, and was very attentive to my wants and feelings. He was divorced and currently living with his mother because he was having a house built at the time. He was eight years older than me, but I didn't mind because I always liked older men. During the course of our relationship, we did many things together. We constantly went to dinner and outings. We would walk on the beach, go bowling, skating, concerts, comedy shows, have picnics, and take weekend vacations. He would even surprise me with little cards and gifts sporadically. I really enjoyed being with him, and it was obvious that our feelings were mutual. He made me happy. We talked about getting married, raising a family, and moving into the house that he was having built. He was anxious to get married soon and wanted children right away. I loved him, but I was not as anxious to marry as he was. I was only 26 years old and wanted to be triple sure that we were doing the right thing at that time. After all, it hadn't been a year since we were dating, and he was already talking marriage. I felt that we needed to continue getting to know each other for a while.

THE PERFECT COUPLE

Most thought that we were the perfect couple, and he made no secret about how he felt about me in the presence of others. He was very good to me. He valued and respected me and truly cared for my feelings, my aspirations, and my goals. But he had a dark side. He was very possessive and had a habit of pushing, grabbing, or shoving me when he would get angry. He wouldn't punch or slap me, but he would still put his hands on me in that manner. He would get upset over what seemed to me to be very petty things such as other people conversing with me; not only men, but women too. He would become extremely angry if anyone of the opposite sex would hug me, even though he would be standing right there. The hugs were very innocent and even though he would be right there, he still did not like it. Whenever someone approached me, I always introduced that person to Robert to make him feel comfortable. I knew that he was very jealous and although I tried to make him feel secure, I would still get the heat from him when people would hug me after church, so I stopped allowing men to hug me. He then started answering the telephone at my apartment and became very controlling. He became jealous if I would talk to my sister or anyone else too long on the telephone, so everyone eventually stopped calling.

As time passed, I started seeing more and more of his dark and ugly side. Our first really bad argument was during the summer on a day that I had been home all day doing nothing but reading and watching television. The phone had not rung except for when he would call to check on me from work. On this particular day when he got off, he called to say that he was on his way over. The minute he knocked on the door, my telephone rang but I answered the door first. He walked into my apartment and went straight to answer the telephone. It was Bill, an old friend who I had not spoken with in a long time. He was just calling to say hello. Robert questioned him, cursed him, and told him never to call my house again. I tried to explain to Robert that I had not spoken with Bill in months and that he was a plutonic friend who I had never dated. He did not believe me, and accused me of talking to men on the phone all day while he was at work. He grabbed and pushed me against the kitchen wall. He was so angry that he took the porcelain collectibles that were on my coffee table and threw them all over my living room. I was so scared that I went to my bedroom and climbed into the bed as he was destroying my apartment. I had never seen that side of him before.

I had some understanding of a man's ego, and I strategically tried to cater to his. I had no fear of competition from other women because he made me feel secure so I tried to do the same for him to no avail. He had a bad temper that often got out of control. After he would cool off, he would apologize and tell me that he loved me. He would then buy me roses or take me on a vacation to make up for what had happened. That soon became very old. I had gotten tired of trying to make him feel secure when I was doing absolutely nothing to make him feel insecure. Everyone had stopped calling me because of him, and I was no longer happy. Finally, I prayed. My prayer to God was: "...*if this man is not the man that you have ordained for me, then please remove him out of my life.*"

I had gotten tired of the constant arguing, and I knew that it was just a matter of time before we dissolved the relationship. During our last argument, he hit me in my face, and I said, "*You have hit me one last time.*" He asked me what that meant and I said, "*It means exactly what you think it means.*" We broke up that day, which was the very next day after I had prayed that specific prayer. He called a few days later apologizing and asking if we could work things out. He reminded me that we had made plans to marry and raise a family. He asked me why I was willing to throw all of that away when we both loved each other. I was adamant in my decision and I told him that I really did not think things were going to work out for us in the future.

PAIN OF A BROKEN HEART

As the days turned into weeks, I began to really miss him. I called him and talked about reconciling. His attitude was very nonchalant, and he was totally not interested in talking to me. Needless-to-say, I was very shocked, considering this was the man who had showered me with love, went over and beyond to please and satisfy me, would buy me cards and roses for no reason and was relentless in trying to marry me. I couldn't believe that he had such a drastic change of heart. I had a hard time dealing with his attitude change so I began to continuously call him. When I realized that he was serious, the pain in my heart surfaced. It was one thing for me to break up with him, but it was quite another for him not to want to be with me. That was rejection and I did not handle rejection well. My heart was broken. The pain was unbearable and indescribable. I cried out to the Lord everyday to heal my broken heart. I began to lose a significant amount of weight. It was so significant that one could see the bones in my face. I couldn't eat, and the little that I did eat was not enough to make me gain weight. I only went to work and back home. I stopped going to church. I wanted to call him, but I didn't. The feeling that I was annoying him when he answered the phone was the thing that stopped me from calling him. There were times that I would sit by the phone, stare at it, and hope that it would ring and be him on the other end. The pain in my heart hurt so badly. I just wanted it to go away. As the days turned into weeks and the weeks into months and the months into years, my heart was still broken. I cried and cried. I couldn't eat or sleep. I had sunk into a depression. I didn't want to be with anyone else but him. I made myself believe that I was in love with him and that I had a broken heart. It was all an illusion.

GETTING THROUGH THE PAIN

As I look back and reflect now, I realize that I was not hurt because I loved him so much. I was hurt because of the rejection. If he and I would have reconciled and I would have broken up with him again, I would have been just fine, but since he was the one who rejected me, that was a devastating blow to my self-esteem, self-confidence, and self-worth. It took me every bit of five years to get him completely out of my system, mind, body, and spirit. The first two and a half years were really hard and very lonely because I would not date anyone else. I stayed home secluded in my apartment. After work and especially during weekends, I did nothing but cry myself to sleep. The pain was still so fresh and so real, and it hurt so bad. It did not seem to be getting better. I needed to focus my thoughts on something positive. I enrolled in school to work on a Masters Degree. Two evenings a week and one full Saturday had me in school. The days I was not in school, I did homework. This was very productive for me because my thoughts were now diverted to something other than the pain from being rejected.

Robert called me one Saturday morning about a year and a half after we broke up. He seemed to be nervous but happy to hear my voice. He stated that he needed to discuss something very important with me. He asked if he could see me that day. At the time of his call, I was headed for school, but I did not tell him where I was going. I said that I was on my way out and that he could call me later if he'd like. Although I was surprised to hear from him, and was still struggling to heal from our breakup, I did not stay on the phone to hold a conversation with him. My tone was very indifferent and I deliberately acted as though I didn't care to speak with him. I did not say that, but my tone did. Needless-to-say, he did not call back until a year later. He revealed the reason why he had called a year before. He had gotten someone pregnant and was confused about the circumstances surrounding the situation. He wanted to know if I still loved and wanted to be with him because that would have been the deciding factor to whether or not he would marry the young lady. He indicated that he loved and missed me immensely, but that his pride did not allow him to return back to me since I had rejected him. According to him, my actions on the phone a year before, helped him to make his decision. He had always told me that if he ever got anyone pregnant, he would marry that person. I don't think he wanted to marry the young lady who was pregnant with his child. She already had a son, and she wasn't the type of woman that I know he was attracted to. Nevertheless, he did marry her and had a baby girl.

THE RELEASE

Years later, he came to visit me at the school where I was teaching. Seeing him after all of those years was weird. I was on the telephone talking to a parent when I looked up and saw him walking around the corner. I ended the call with the parent and greeted him in a friendly manner. He put his arms around me and would not let go. I had to push him away. We talked for a few minutes and exchanged pleasantries. I was married at the time and told him that I was *happily* married (which was a lie) and had a son. He bragged about his daughter, and felt the need to remind me that he had gotten married and had a big wedding. I said to him, *"You did the right thing by marrying her when she was pregnant with your child."* I know that my statement wasn't nice, but I felt that it wasn't nice of him to brag about his wedding either, especially when he and I had so many conversations about how *our* wedding was going to be. I did not want to continue the conversation, so I explained that I had to return to my classroom to teach my students. They were in Physical Education at the time but he did not know it. He hugged me again, and asked me if I missed him. My response was, *"That doesn't matter because I am married now."* He left. I had finally gotten my release. After he left, I realized that I was completely over him because there were no feelings that surfaced in me when I saw him that day. I felt nothing when he hugged me and I was even turned off by his looks. He had shaved his mustache, and that was a complete turn off to me. I was finally over him!

I can look back and really laugh now. It's amazing how when we are in relationships, we don't see anything wrong with the person that we profess to love so much, but when we are no longer in love, we can sure see clearly. After the fact, we say things like this: *"Girl, I saw Robert today and he looks bad. He shaved his mustache, walks with a limp, has a huge flat nose, a bald spot, crooked teeth, and bad breath. Girl he is all messed up."* The reality is that he looked just like that when you dated him, but now that you are no longer in love and can see clearly, you can see all his flaws (Robert did not have those flaws, but you get my point). A man's conversation might sound something like this: *Man, I saw Mia today and she sure doesn't look like she looked when I dated her. Everything about her is fake. She had fake hair, fake eyes, and fake nails. She also had crossed eyes and facial hair.* But the truth is that, girlfriend looked like that when you dated her and all your friends knew it. You shared the same razor with her. But now that you are no longer in love, she isn't all that you thought she was.

It's amazing what time does. It not only heals wounds, but it brings about change. Thank God for experiences, for they are our best teacher. I have no regrets for having had a broken heart and falling in love. At least I know what both feel like. It would be nice if the falling in love part could last forever. Who knows, maybe it can with the right person. But I will not cry because it's over, but laugh and be thankful because it happened. Walk in wisdom. Laugh at your experiences, be grateful for them and laugh at the world.

~~ LESSONS LEARNED ~~

1. We cannot shield ourselves from rejection. Rejection is only destructive when you internalize it and allow it to creep into your belief system. The forces of evil love to fuel the fires of low-self esteem with different forms of rejection. But if we accept rejection as a part of human experience, we can take every negative situation and become a stronger person from it.

2. Some people have never had the opportunity to be in love. Some people have never had a broken heart. I was blessed to have experienced both. Now, I can encourage someone else as they go through the same things.

~~REFLECTION QUESTIONS~~

1. Do you appreciate the experience of having had a broken heart or are you still holding on to yesterday and allowing yourself to continue feeling the pain? Have you released the person to whom the broken heart is associated?

2. Are you still holding on to the successes or failures from the past or have you learned to laugh at them so they can finally vanish in order to make room for present possibilities?

Chapter

5

Control Your Emotions in Every Situation
Playing With Fire May Get You Burned

All nature is a circle of moods, and I am a part of nature and so like the tides, my moods will rise, my moods will fall.

I will remember that every adversity carries with it the seed of tomorrow's victory and every sadness carries with it the seed of tomorrow's joy. I will master my emotions so that each day will be positive, for unless my mood is right, my day will be a failure. I will do this by learning the secret of the ages: "Weak is she who allows her thoughts to control her actions; Strong is she who forces her actions to control her thoughts."

Each day when I awaken, I will follow this plan of battle before I let the forces of sadness, self-pity, and failure capture me:

When I feel depressed, I will sing.
When I feel sad, I will laugh.
When I feel sick, I will double my labor.
When I feel inferior, I will wear new clothes.
When I feel uncertain, I will ask questions.
When I feel poverty, I will think of the wealth to come.
When I feel incompetent, I will remember past successes.

If I feel insignificant, I will remember my goals.

Those such as depression and sadness are easy to recognize, but there are others that approach with a smile and the hand of friendship, and they too can deceive me. Against them, I must never relinquish control. Therefore, I will remember the following:

When I feel overconfident, I will recall my failures.
When I overindulge, I will think of past hungers.
When I feel complacency, I will remember my competition.
When I feel moments of greatness, I will remember moments of shame.
When I attain great wealth, I will remember those in poverty
When I feel overly proud, I will remember a moment of weakness.

Remembering these moments will keep my life balanced. With this new knowledge, I will understand and recognize the moods of others whom I encounter and I will make allowances for his or her anger and irritation of the day, for they know not the secret of controlling their thoughts. From this moment, I am prepared to control whatever personality awakes me each day. I will master my moods through positive action, and when I master my moods, I control my destiny. Today I control my destiny, and my destiny is to fulfill God's perfect will for my life.

NEVER SAY NEVER

Through experience I have learned to, "never say never". I had heard stories of women and their awful experiences with men. I had heard of instances where men had used women for money, ran up credit cards bills, beat them, verbally abused them, cheated on them, driven other women around town in their cars, etc. As I would listen to these women tell of their horrible experiences, I would distinctively remember thinking how stupid they were and how desperate for a man they must have been to allow those things to happen to them. I was always quick to judge and say that if a man did not have anything intellectually, financially, or spiritually to contribute to what I had acquired, I would never get involved with him. It was not until I experienced first hand what it was like to be used, disrespected, abused, and disgraced that I realized it could happen to anyone.

We are not forced to give in to temptation. We can either succumb or we can resist. We make our own choices, and we must live with the consequences of the choices we make. I will never forget that Wednesday afternoon in 1996 when I was in Burger King on my lunch break. I felt very uncomfortable being stared at, but I tried to ignore it. The man finally approached me and said, *"How are you? My name is Victor. I'm sorry for staring at you, but I think you are gorgeous."* I responded in a very nonchalant way and said, *"Thank you"* continuing to review the menu. Victor proceeded to say, *"If you don't mind, may I have your name and phone number so that I may keep in contact with you?"* Again, very curt, I said, *"No, you may not have my number."* And I continued looking up at the menu. The persistent man then said, *"Well, here's my number. If you get some time, give me a call".* Aggravated at that point, I said, *"Don't waste your time, because I won't be calling you. Have a nice day."* I had just gotten out of a bad relationship and was still

63

trying get over that, therefore I did not want to talk to or get involved with anyone else. I just wanted to be left alone. He then walked out of the restaurant. Walking back to my car with the food, I noticed that Victor was still in the parking lot. He said, *"Oh, I see you like red too."* He had a red Nissan 300zx. I had a red Mitsubishi Eclipse. I did not respond. I got into my car and drove off.

SO WE MEET AGAIN

Approximately 8 months later, while in the grocery store, a man began walking toward me on the same aisle in which I was shopping. As he was walking by, I stared at him because I knew him from somewhere. He turned to me and said, *"Is there a problem?"* I said, *"Yes, I know you from somewhere."* He said, *"Yea, I'm the one that you were very rude to in Burger King."* Instinctively, I began laughing. Naturally, that broke the ice. I was not rude to him this time and I noticed that he was a fairly decent looking guy. He spoke well and seemed very charming and mannerable. He was nicely dressed and had a nice physique. We exchanged phone numbers, and he called me as soon as I arrived home from shopping. I gathered from talking to him that he lived with his brother and was unemployed. He stated that he was a recording artist awaiting a record contract. He told me that he could not get a regular job because it interfered with his singing career since he needed to be in the studio working on his next album. He went on to say that he had a significant amount of money saved up for bills and that he was financially secure. He called almost everyday thereafter and was insistent on coming to my apartment. He eventually stopped calling when I would not allow him to come over. Between the time that he stopped calling until I spoke with him again was about three months.

One day, while home alone, or should I say lonely, I decided to give him a call on his beeper. Without delay, he started asking if he could come over, so this time I allowed him to do so. He no longer had the Nissan, but was driving a very nice Lincoln Town Car. He told me that he had traded in the Nissan because it was too small and he needed extra room for his two daughters who were elementary aged at the time. While at my apartment, we talked for a while, then he left. Although I was single, he was not the caliber of man that I was use to dating or one with whom I would consider having a relationship. Even though he was decent-looking, charming, well spoken, and seemed to be very mannerable, there was something sinister and dark about him that I could not put my finger on. It did not really matter however, because he did not appeal to me. He was someone to talk to and pass the time. He had nothing to offer me spiritually, financially, or intellectually, and I knew I could never get serious with someone of his caliber. I allowed him to entertain me because there was no one else in my life at the time, and I soon learned that when you play with fire, you get burned.

THE TRUTH COMES OUT

As I reflect back, I remember how he used to ask me questions such as, *"If I needed a place to stay, would you help me?"* That is not a typical everyday question that people ask when you meet them. That question alone should have told me half the story of his life. Because of the fact that I had allowed myself to spend too much time with Victor, I had sex with him and became pregnant. It was not soon thereafter, I found out that he did not live with his brother, but he in-fact lived with a woman. The woman somehow found my phone number and began calling me leaving strange messages and hanging up. I also learned that his red Nissan had been repossessed and the

65

woman with whom he was living had financed the Lincoln Town car for him in her name. He began asking to "borrow" money to make the car note, pay the car insurance and buy things for his daughters. I loaned him the money when he asked for it. I honestly thought that there was a record contract forthcoming as he had told me, and that he would be able to help out financially when the baby arrived. I also expected the money that I had been loaning him to be repaid. I had never had a man ask me for money before, and I felt strange about it at first, but I figured it had to take a lot of courage for a man to ask a woman to borrow money. Therefore, I figured he must have really needed it. I was used to dating stable, accomplished men with gainful employment, so this was new to me. I thought that he was just going through some hard times as everyone does at some point in life. I believed in helping people when and if I could. However, I soon began to see that he was taking my kindness for weakness.

WHO IS THIS WOMAN?

In the meantime, I was carrying his child. The woman continued calling and asking me questions, none of which I would answer. She would call and ask to speak with him. I would tell her that he was not home. She would then ask, *"Who are you to Victor?"* I would hang up. On another occasion she asked, *"Are you Rodney's girlfriend?"* I would hang up. Finally, she decided to be straightforward and talk to me like a mature adult. She told me that her name was Jennifer and said that my so-called man was her man. She proceeded to tell me that Victor and her had been living together, but that he never came home claiming he had to sleep in the studio at nights. She explained that she had financed the Lincoln Town Car for him, but that he was in arrears with the car payments. She went on to complain that he did not contribute financially to her household expenses, ran up her home and cellular telephone bills, ate all of her groceries, and was leeching off of her. She continued to tell me that Victor had disrespected her constantly by having other women call there for him. According to her, he talked to women directly in her face and would tell her that the conversations were business. She warned me that he was an compulsive liar and that she constantly baby-sat his daughters while he would be elsewhere. She said that he would come home at five and six o' clock in the morning and would say that he had been in the studio all night. She also claimed that she would buy food, school clothes, Christmas toys, and birthday gifts for his daughters and spent more time with them than he would. When I told her that I was five months pregnant from him, she told me that she had been pregnant from him twice, but had miscarried one and aborted one. She was not disrespectful during the conversation, but seemed to be more angry and hurt than anything else. I was calm while speaking with her and we were very cordial. I was almost to the point of being apathetic. I told her that she could have him back because he had been nothing but a financial and psychological burden to me. Surprisingly, she said that she loved him, but that she was not going to be played for a fool by him any longer. She may not have realized it at the time, but she made a very wise decision in leaving him alone. She should thank God that she had no connections to him that a baby would have required.

INVASION

There came a time for me to visit my sister in Tallahassee, where she attended school. The day that I was supposed to leave, I inadvertently locked myself out of the apartment and had to go to the rental office to get a duplicate key. I did not have time to take the key back to the rental office, so I asked Victor if he would take it back for me because the people at the rental office were very adamant about returning their keys. I went to Tallahassee and stayed there for a week. When I returned, I discovered that Victor never returned the key, but had used it to move all of his belongings into my apartment. He no longer had the Lincoln Town Car or any car for that matter. Jennifer had put him out and taken her car back. I guess I did not mind him moving in because I did want to be with or "appear" to be with the father of my child although I did not love him. However, the way he moved in was deceitful, especially since I had been speaking with him from Tallahassee and he never mentioned a word about it. He had deliberately kept my apartment key so that he could have access in and out while I was in Tallahassee. When I returned, he began driving my car and staying out with it for two and three days at a time without calling me. The first time he did that, I was worried and actually called the police to report a missing person. I could not fathom a man leaving a pregnant woman home alone for three days with no transportation and no contact. That was incomprehensible to me. When I approached him about coming in at 4:00 o' clock in the morning and staying out for days at a time, his reply to me was that he was grown and nobody could tell him when and what time he needed to come home.

Without my permission, he had a sound system installed in my car, filled my trunk with speakers, and had my cassette player removed and replaced with a compact disc player. I was very upset about that, and I expressed it to him because at the time, I did not own one cd, and I listened to cassette tapes when I would drive my car. Needless-to-say, he never put the cassette player back in. He would be gone for days at a time with my car leaving me stranded with no where to go. Oftentimes I would be stranded in the house with no way of going anywhere. He would not return my pages and I had to cancel doctor appointments as a result of not having a way to get there. All I did was make the car payments because I never drove my own car anymore. He almost never slept at the apartment at night and I almost never saw him. His excuse was always that he had to be in the studio for days at a time so he slept there at night, but when I would call the studio, I was always told that he wasn't there.

MEETING HIS DAUGHTERS

The time came for me to meet his little girls. He had one biological daughter and claimed her sister as his own. Their mother had previously been a stripper and had three children from three different men. She was not married and rarely spent time with her children. They were always with other people, and in my opinion, neglected. One evening, he brought the older two girls to the apartment without informing me of their coming. He dropped them off and said that they were spending the night. He then said that he was leaving to go to the studio. So I asked him who was going to baby-sit them. He boldly said, *"You."* After leaving, he did not call nor return back for two days. They would ask me where their father was, and I did not know what to say. The oldest one was nine at the time and the other one was seven. One would think that since his daughters were there, he would have at least called to check on them. He never did. I learned very quickly that Victor was an inconsiderate, trifling, selfish liar who had no regard for anyone other than himself.

THE LEECH

The rare times that Victor came home, he would talk to women on my phone directly in front of me. I would look at him as if he was crazy, but I did not open my mouth. I remember thinking in my mind, *"Does this man really believe that I am just that gullible and dumb that he would actually sit in my face and talk to other women?* I never questioned him or said a word. I was planning my leave from him after the baby. He ran up my telephone bill every month with long distance calls, causing the phone bill to be over $170 a month. Prior to that, I had never paid more than $40 per month. Needless-to-say, he never contributed a dime towards the bill. When I would show the bill to him, he would not mention anything about paying it. But he continued running it up to the point that it was disconnected. Without contributing a dime to groceries, he ate all the food in my kitchen. I would buy food, but when I would go in the kitchen to eat something, everything would literally be gone from gallons of ice cream, entire packs of cookies, loaves of bread, packs of lunchmeat, everything! That was extremely frustrating for me, especially since I was pregnant. One would think that since he knew he had not contributed a dime towards groceries, he would have used a bit of constraint when eating. This man was a parasite with no respect for women and had no home training. He was the perfect example of how boys turn out to be when they have no positive male role models in their lives to look up to. Victor had no wisdom and was oblivious to how women should be treated. He was one of those men who hunted for established women with good paying jobs, credit cards, money in the bank, and good credit, so that he could charm his way into their lives and leech off of them. It is so sad that there are so many single women who want and deserve a good man, but compromise their values and expectations for men like Victor. Unfortunately, they eventually find themselves in relationships that tear down their sense of self-worth. I guess I was one of them. Such non-affirming relationships can be devastating.

IS THIS REALLY HAPPENING?

I was in a state of shock experiencing these things as a result of this man. I really could not believe that a person could be so trifling. I was used to being wined and dined by well-established dignified men who cared for me emotionally, affectionately, and intellectually. I had dated men who cared for my feelings and respected me like a lady should be respected. I had never had a man use me or even ask to borrow money. To go from that to this was a major and drastic change. Everything that Jennifer had told me about him became my living reality. He was a habitual liar. Ninety-eight percent of everything that came out of his mouth was a lie. I honestly believe that since I never questioned him about anything, never raised my voice, never argued or caused a problem while I was pregnant, he assumed that I was naïve and gullible. He thought that I was the sweetest, nicest, lady that a man could have to walk all over. That was not the case. I had mastered my emotions because of my unborn baby. I was only exercising calmness because I was carrying a child. I am a firm believer that one's actions and feelings can have a devastating affect on their unborn child leaving lasting impressions on that child's subconscious mind, which causes unexplained mental tendencies and behaviors later on in that child's life. Therefore, I tried not to bring any stress on myself.

He did nothing to financially prepare for the baby's arrival. He caused me nothing but problems and was a huge financial and psychological burden on me. Once, the FBI came to the apartment complex looking for him for possession of stolen property. There were so many other incidents that made me realize that I had really gotten myself caught up with a con artist and common thug. The mistake of associating with this man was bigger than I had realized, and I asked myself over and over how I could have gotten so deeply entangled with this caliber of a man. Depression had started to creep in, but I recognized it and fought it off by praying and reading the Bible.

THE EARLY ARRIVAL

Time was approaching for me to have the baby and I had secretly arranged to move into a two-bedroom condominium alone. Everything was finalized and Victor had no knowledge of it. I had planned to have some male friends do the moving for me while he was gone on one of his three or four day excursions. Everything was ready. After the move, I was not going to contact him because of the baby, but initially, I knew that I needed to be away from him. I thought that since he was gone 95% of the time, he would not be there when it to contact him for a while. I knew that at some point, I had to co was time for me to give birth. After all, I very seldom paged him, but the few times I did, he never returned the calls. I had my plans ready to leave this man, but it did not happen quite the way I planned.

My baby girl decided to come a month early, and it just so happened that Victor had been home for about 20 minutes (from being gone three days) when my water broke. So yes, he was right there when I gave birth to Stephanie. She was such a precious and delightful sight. She looked so angelic as I stared into her tiny face. Looking at her seemed to eradicate all that I had been going through prior to her arrival. So many emotions emerged when the nurse placed her in my arms. The love seemed to spring forth as I held her and admired her beauty. From that moment on, I was only focused on caring for and protecting that innocent child. Nothing else mattered.

However, Stephanie's early arrival put a monkey wrench in my moving plans. Victor found out about those plans and certainly planned on coming right along. After all, he did not have a place to live, no job, no car of his own, and no money. I guess the woman he had been sleeping with only allowed him there for a couple days at a time. After I brought Stephanie home, he insisted that *"we"* move right away. I knew that he wanted to move because the FBI had been watching the apartment complex and was looking for him.

It was nothing but hell in the condo with him. The same things were happening, but to a greater degree. The situation was exacerbated because I was no longer pregnant, and I began to voice my anger and aggravation towards how I felt about him. Everything I had been holding inside came out in very hostile, cruel, and wicked ways. He still had not paid a bill, but was still running up bills, staying out for days at a time, stealing money from me, eating all the groceries, talking to women on my telephone, running up the electricity bill with the air-conditioner, utilizing the washing machine and dryer with only one and two articles of clothing in the machine, having women call my home, and taking my car for days at a time.

LOSING CONTROL

After three months of living in the condominium, he told me that he wanted his daughters to move in - permanently. I asked, *"Who is going to take care of them?"* His response was, *"us."* I then said *"How are [we] going to take care of them, when [I] am the only one who works?"* I told him that they could not live there, and I was very adamant about that, and made it very clear.

I was totally miserable and I had allowed him to bring my spirits and character down to street-woman mentality. I did not care anymore. I would curse at him so loud that I am sure the entire complex could hear it. I had lost total respect for him and total control of myself. The sight of him disgusted me. I would say things to him that no self-respecting woman should ever say

73

to a man, or anybody else for that matter. The tongue is a powerful tool that can be used for good or evil. Words have power, and I was using my words to speak negativity and death into his life from every fiber in my body. My words were lethal. There was so much hatred inside me for this man, that I would tell him to do me and the baby a favor and go catch a bullet in the head. That is how poisonous my words were. My personality had drastically changed for the worse. Almost every word that came out of my mouth towards him was profanity. My personal life was even reflected in my job. I had become a negative person who saw the negativity in everything. Misery loves company. I had allowed this man to bring out every repulsive, evil, and horrible characteristic in me. Being with him was a disgrace. One of my close friends called me crying when she found out that her sister had had sex with him. As a friend, she felt that she needed to tell me. I appreciated her honesty and sincerity, but at that point, I did not care who he slept with because I wasn't sleeping with him. I just wanted him out of my life. During their lunchtime, some of the teachers I worked with would see him driving around other women in my car. An associate of mine who worked at another school called to ask if I was still with Victor because she knew his new "girlfriend". She told me that Victor came to the beauty salon quite frequently (in my car) to see the girlfriend where she worked. She said that she knew my car and recognized him to be the man who dropped me off to work. She said that when she told the girl, *"That's my friend's husband"*, the woman said, *"Not anymore, he's divorced"*. That was not the case. I was humiliated because I knew that everything I was being told was true, and that I was being talked about. I knew that people must have thought I was desperate for a man to have been with him. These were the same thoughts I had about other women when I would hear of things their boyfriends or husbands had done to them, so I knew that people were thinking and saying the same things about me. What goes around comes around, thoughts, words, and deeds. After the many reports of people seeing him all over town in my car while I would be at work, I stopped him from driving me to work. It was already embarrassing to have him dropping me off in my own car because I had that car long before I met him and everyone knew it, so for him to drop me off to work, people had to know that he did not have a car of his own. After I stopped him from driving my car, he hated the fact that it would be sitting in the parking lot all day while I was at work because he felt he could be driving it. While I was working, he would be soaking up the air-conditioner, running up the electricity bill and talking on the phone. I had to have a lock put on my bedroom door because of his stealing. I also had to lock laundry detergent and certain non-perishable food items in my room so that I could have a snack when I desired one and had items to use when I needed to.

I expressed to him many times that I wanted him to move out. I tried being mature about it when I first asked him to move, not realizing that I was not dealing with a mature adult. My spirits were so low because I wanted this man completely out of my life and it did not seem like he was going anywhere. The baby did not change things at all. In fact, he got worse after she was born. There were no benefits with him in my life, not for me, not for my daughter. For him, there were many benefits. He was living rent free, paid no bills, driving a car without making a car-payment, had a bed to sleep in, food to eat, stealing money, unlimited phone access, and the leisure of coming in and out as he pleased. Why would anyone want to leave that? It was very hard getting rid of him to say the very least.

ROOM 203

One Saturday morning as I was lying down in my bedroom at the condo, Victor was in the living room on the phone talking to one of his female acquaintances. I had heard him asking for room 203 many times, and I was already fed up, so I got up and asked him to take out the garbage. He told the woman that he would call her back, but that he would be there shortly. When he walked out of the house, I pressed the redial button and wrote down the phone number. She was expecting him to come over, so he eventually left. While he was gone, I called the number, and it happened to be the number to a motel called *The Vagabond Motel* (go figure). I asked for room 203. No one answered in the room the first time I called. When I called back, I asked the attendant if there was a room in the name of Victor Thomas. The attendant told me that the room was previously in two names, Victor's name and another name, but that Victor's name had been recently removed. He went on to explain that the room had been in Victor's name for about seven months until the recent switch (it is amazing how people willingly give out information). Later on, I called back and asked for room 203 again. This time a female answered. So I, (being the drama queen that I am), pretended to be calling from the motel's hospitality office with a few questions regarding her motel stay. After asking the preliminary questions such as how satisfied she was with the stay, would she be likely to refer someone to the motel, would she return back, etc., I mentioned how I noticed the recent name change under which the room was in. The woman informed me that the room had been in her boyfriend, Victor's name, but that she had his name removed so that she could add her new roommate's name instead, who had just come in town to stay with her. When I asked if she would be checking out soon, she stated that she did not know. She told me that she lived out of town and anticipated being at the motel for a while. I immediately perceived that she was an exotic dancer who had been living in the motel for quite some time. I decided to pay a little visit to room 203 when Victor returned with my car. As I approached the motel door, I could hear loud music playing from the outside of the room. A very rough-looking female with many scars on her face answered the door in a bad wig, a T-shirt and no bottoms. I was a bit startled at first sight of her because she looked like a man trying to imitate a woman. After I told her who I was, she seemed a bit intimidated, but answered my questions regarding Victor. She told me that he was only a friend of hers who frequently came to visit with some of his other friends to "hang out" with her and her (stripper) friends. She added that there was nothing going on between the two of them. She seemed to be fumbling over her words a whole lot, however. While she was talking to me, I was trying to figure out if she was a man or a real woman. I finally concluded that she was a real woman.

When I returned back home, Victor was sitting on the couch with a nasty attitude and angry look on his face because she had called him and apparently did not tell him what she had told me. She told him that she had confessed to me about the two of them. What he did not know is that she lied for him and I still did not know the whole truth. He was the one who confirmed their relationship. I did not say a word to him when I walked in the house. I checked on my baby, fed her, and cooked dinner. I fed his daughters who were there, was preparing a plate of food for myself and was just about to sit down and eat, when the phone rang. It was my mother. She told me that Victor had called her and told her that I went to the home of one of his friends, confronted the man's wife, and accused her of sleeping with Victor. I did not appreciate my mother calling me and questioning me about what went on under my roof between the father of my child and myself. Furthermore, when he called her, I felt that she should have told him that he needed to work out his problems with me and that she did not want to get involved. Instead of doing that, she had the audacity to question me about a lie that he told her. I was extremely angered by her phone call, especially since I had never been close to her and did not share things with her. I had always been a private person, and I did not permit many people into my personal business, not even her. So, when she questioned me about that, I proceeded to tell her the truth, although it was none of her business. It was very typical of him to come home after being gone for days, get on the phone, call family members and fabricate outlandish stories about me. In a distorted way, I think he did that to alleviate the guilt from what he had been doing in the streets. Those things were, at the time unforgivable to me. In my mind, a man who speaks lies and negativity about his woman, can never be trusted. In my eyes, a man should be his woman's best friend and greatest protector. He should defend her honor, and not allow anyone to speak derogatory about her. This man was the extreme opposite of what I thought a man should be. In fact, he was a poor excuse for a man. It takes an evil and malicious person to make up lies about another person in an effort to make himself or herself look good. I had been very good to this man, and there was no justification for the lies that he told about me. Assassinating my character, misrepresenting my motives, and trying to taint my image were typical things that Victor had done to me, and it really did hurt, especially since I had done nothing but try and help him. Lies always hurt.

When I hung up from speaking with my mother, he said, *"Yo stupid ass out there running the streets questioning females like you straight out the ghetto!"* My response: *"You hang out in sleazy motels with low-life strippers as if you are from the ghetto.* His response: *"She's a better woman than you!"* My response: *She probably got AIDS!* His response: *"If she got it, you got it!"* The plate that was in my hand was thrown in his face with a side order of broken plate pieces to go, because he then had to get out of my house. This led into an extremely violent domestic altercation in front of his children and my baby, which ended with the police at my front door. When they came, he was arrested because there was a bench warrant for his arrest for having a suspended license and not paying for speeding tickets. After he was taken to jail, his daughters were still at my house, so I called their mother to come and pick them up. She never did, even after my persistent phone calls. What kind of woman would leave her children someplace after she had been called, told what happened, and asked to come and pick them up?

As I thought about the situation, I began questioning myself. Although I did not love him, and I knew he did not love me, I couldn't help but wonder what it was about me that turned him off to the point that he had to turn to a woman who looked like a man. I felt horrible. If I would have beheld a beautiful or even decent-looking woman on the other side of that motel door, I would have had to step up my game a notch, and maybe even for the sake of pride only, tried to fight for him, but after seeing the kind of woman that he was drawn to, it gave me a deep reality check of the type of man this really was. What real man would want that caliber of woman? What kind of man was this?

After he was released from jail, I did not want him coming back to my house. I had the locks changed and asked him to send someone to get his possessions so that I would have no further dealings with him. He had not done one thing for me or my newborn, and she was then two months old. He had not even purchased one pack of Pampers for her. He called everyone that he could from jail, begging them to talk to me, telling them that he loved me and wanted to be with me and his baby daughter. No one had any knowledge of all the things this man had already taken me through. They did not know that he was a leech, a womanizer, a user, and a con-artist because I was very private and never told anyone what I had been going through with him.

I was also too embarrassed to tell anybody. I let his oldest sister and my mother convince me that I should take him back because they said my daughter needed both parents. They explained that it was not easy raising a child alone, no relationship was easy and that I should aim towards making it work. But I was already taking care of the baby alone. He was never there and never did one thing to help support her. And as far as the relationship goes... what relationship? I received lectures and speeches from well-meaning people on why I should take him back and like a fool, I did. Of course, he apologized, cried like a baby, and swore that he would never cheat again, lie again, would get a job, start paying bills, and take care of his baby. They were all lies. After two weeks, it was the same cycle all over again. He was just a little bit more discreet, but still sloppy with his disloyalty and infidelity.

SAME STUFF DIFFERENT DAY

He continued to stay out for days at a time, would come home in the daytime and continued his relationship with the stripper. It was commonplace for him to come in the house at five in the morning and go directly to the guest bedroom after having been gone for days. How could a person be gone so long then come in the house and go directly to the guest bedroom? I could have been cut up, beat up, raped, or even murdered in the next room. He would never have known it because he never checked on us. After having had sex with other women and being gone for so long, his guilt would not allow him to even come and check on me or the baby in the next room. After three weeks had passed since he was back from jail, he said to me during an argument, *"She's no longer in a motel, she has her own apartment now, and it's very nice."*

The day that he was arrested, I called her and asked her why she lied to me. She was bold, belligerent, loud, cantankerous, and very slick with her mouth over the telephone, totally different from how she had been in person. I threatened her and I'm sure she took me seriously. I did not do it because she was seeing him. I threatened her because of the disrespectful tone in which she was speaking to me. During the course of the conversation, she told me that Victor picked her up every night from the club where she danced and would stay with her all night. Her exact words to me were, *"He sleeps with me every night."* This, I knew had to be true because it was very consistent with him never being home at night. In addition, she said that he had been doing it for almost a year. This statement also had to be true, because he had never been home with me while I was pregnant, nor was he home with me after his baby was born. The woman was very confident when telling me these things because she knew they were true. The feeling that I picked up from her was this: *"If he loved or even respected you, he would spend his nights with you, but he is always with me."* She never said it, but it was clearly indicative in her voice.

This woman was seemingly uneducated and had a vernacular consisting of profanity and very poor grammar. However, she conveyed herself to me quite clearly, and I knew exactly where she was coming from. She also told me that whenever she called him, he knew to come, which was consistent with his pager going off, him immediately calling her back, and then leaving the house. I was not upset with her, because I was at the point to where I had lost total respect for him and really didn't care. But I asked her why she felt that she had to lie to me when I came there. When she said to me, *"I don't have to tell you a Goddamn thang."* that's when I told her that if she cherished her life at all, she would not go back to that motel that night, and if she did, they would find her body floating in a lake with her tongue missing in the morning. She checked out of the motel the very same day and never returned. So yes, I certainly believed that she had a new apartment.

There were many situations involving other women, some worse than the one I just explained. I didn't care anymore. I just wanted him out of my life and out of my house. I took out a restraining order against him and changed my locks. He would try and come in through the windows four and five o' clock in the morning, yelling for me to unlock the door. People would see him and call the police. He would leave the complex when they arrived and returned when they left. It was a nightmare. He broke my sliding glass doors and windows trying to get in the house and caused me problem after problem. He would steal money from me and also out of his daughter's piggy bank. He would take my house keys out of my purse and hide them so that he could get in the house while I was at work since I had changed the locks and did not give him a key. It was at the point that when I left in the morning, he had to leave. I was living a nightmare. He was a sorry, poor excuse for a man, and I wished over and over that I had never met him. I would go to bed at night and wish that the whole situation was a bad nightmare. When I would wake up and realize that it was real, I would cry. I had become depressed and could feel that I was on the verge of a nervous breakdown.

ABOUT TO EXPLODE

Absolutely no one knew what I was going through. Since I was a private person, I would hold things inside. I was about to explode because I was enduring so much mistreatment, and it seemed as though there was no way out. As close as my sister Lisa and I are, I never told her because she was (and still is) so sensitive, and I knew how she would react. She would cry, then curse, then scream, and go from one extreme to the other. However, I sensed that she knew things weren't right because she made a statement once when I was pregnant. She said that it wasn't good for me to be by myself so much in my condition. Every time she called, I was alone, so she perceived that I was alone a lot. I finally broke down and told Teresa, whom I thought was a friend, but she turned out to be the worst person to tell. She told others what I had been telling her, including my mother, and she also added many lies to the situation, making it worse. We must be very careful about who we choose to divulge personal matters to.

In spite of all that he had taken me through and knowing that he had made me miserable, he still would not leave! I had told him what I thought of him many, many times. I held nothing back. Most men, for the sake of their pride and manhood would have left once they knew that the woman did not want them beyond a shadow of a doubt. Not this man. He was going to stay there and suck all the life out of me. My negative feelings towards him never changed, never fluctuated, nor deviated. They remained consistent. There were no mixed feelings being sent to him. Even when things appeared to be better, I wanted him gone. I was very consistent in conveying daily that I wanted him out. There was no swaying back and forth with me. He knew by no uncertain terms that I wanted him out of my house and life. He would use the baby as an excuse to stay. I knew that I had made a very big mistake when I allowed others to talk me into doing something that I was totally against by allowing him back after the jail incident. I only did it for my daughter, but ultimately, I am the one who had to live with him, not them. My peace of mind is a priority and I should have considered that before letting him back in. Big mistake. Every time I looked into his face, I would see the darkness in his soul. I simply could not get rid of that man because the demon in him was stubborn and strong. He was a bloodsucking leech that I could not shake off.

ON THE EDGE

I was on the verge of a nervous breakdown. The man would not leave. He had never slept seven consistent nights at home. Not even after his baby was born did he stay home. After Stephanie arrived, I had to find work immediately. As a teacher on maternity leave, the school system would not allow me to return back to work before the six weeks was up, so I had to find work elsewhere until I was cleared to return back. I literally had to make him stay home and keep his baby while I worked a temporary job. Why should I have paid a sitter when he sat home all day and did nothing? That was the least he could have done, but he asked me to pay him for keeping his own child. I would have been a bigger fool than I already was had I done that. After I returned back to work, I worked three jobs at one time to stay afloat. I was teaching elementary school during the day, preparing taxes at night during tax season, and teaching college students at the university one night a week. Other than Stephanie, nothing good had come out of my meeting Victor. I had to do what I could to keep a roof over my head, keep food in the house, and care for my baby girl. He was just another mouth to feed. I was literally taking care of a grown man. Stephanie was the only motivation that kept me going from day to day. I awakened every morning and went to work for her. Unfortunately, that motivation soon vanished. Stephanie died at three months old from Sudden Infant Death Syndrome, commonly called SIDS.

I had no more ties to Victor, and so I felt that I finally had way out. After Stephanie's death, I tried talking to him maturely by asking him how long he thought it would take him to move out. He would suck his teeth, take my car keys, and leave. Being in the house alone everyday was dreadfully depressing because my baby was gone. After she died, the grief overwhelmed me, and I had to take a leave of absence from work. While on leave, I received grief counseling. During one session, the counselor told me that I was a positive person who was surrounded by negative people. What was I to do?

Stephanie died on August 29, 1997. After her death, I was oblivious to anything that was happening in the world. It was two weeks later that I learned about Princess Diana's death. The Princess died on August 31, 1997. Mother Teresa died on September 5, 1997. My baby, a princess, and a saint all died within seven days of each other. Stephanie is in good company.

A NIGHTMARE MARRIAGE

In the second week of September, 1997, after Victor came home from having been gone four days, I tried once again talking to him and asking him how soon he thought he could find a place to live. I was very calm when I spoke with him because Stephanie had died, and I was emotionally depleted and did not have the energy to fuss, argue, or yell. I told him again that I did not love him and never did. I expressed the fact that since there were no more ties between us, there was no need in trying to be together. I told him that he had been a burden on me and that my life was extremely unhappy because he was in it. His question to me was, *"Can I be a roommate?"* I explained that roommates pay rent and besides that, I just wanted to be by myself. He became desperate and started talking about marriage. I told him that he was not the type of man that I wanted to marry, and I needed a husband with gainful employment who knew how to pay bills. I also reminded him that I did not love him, which is the foundation of a marriage. This was the first mature and cordial conversation that we had ever had. I was very composed and respectful at this point. For the first time, I think that he really comprehended that from the core of my soul I wanted him

85

out of my life. He told me that if he left, I would have nobody. I told him that if he stayed I would have nobody.

The next day, I had to report to jury duty. Victor came with me and pressured me hard and relentlessly about getting married while we were at the courthouse. The man was desperate. He thought about the conversation that had occurred the day before, the fact that he had nothing, no place to live, no where to go, no job, no car, no money, absolutely nothing, so he figured that if he married me, he could secure those things for himself. Stupid me. I allowed myself to become persuaded to marry him simply because he pressured me hard and I wanted him to shut up. While exchanging vows at the courthouse, I developed a huge knot in my stomach. I knew in my heart and soul that I was marrying the wrong man, and I was screaming inside. I believed that I had just forfeited the man that the Lord had for me, the real man that God destined for me, my soul mate, gone forever. I wanted to vomit. How could I have let myself get into this horrifying situation? How could I get out of this? There was no getting out.

There is nothing worse than giving the right thing to the wrong person. After I was married, I knew that I had to be a faithful and devoted wife, and in order to have a happy marriage, I had to release all that he had done to me in the past and forgive, otherwise, the marriage would be sure to fail. Therefore, I decided to forget every horrible incident that I had experienced with him and focus on the future. I wanted the marriage to work although I knew I didn't love him. I didn't even like him. I had always said that once I got married, I wanted to stay married to the same man until death do us part. I did not believe in divorce. I meant that in my heart. However, when envisioning my marriage, I always imagined being in love and having a simple, yet elegant wedding. I had dreamed about those things since I was a little girl. All of those visions were out the window in five minutes. There would be no wedding, no wedding ring, no love.

After I was married, I said, *"I would like to have a wedding ring."* After all, I had paid for the marriage license and everything else, so I felt that surely he would try to buy me a wedding ring. However, his response to my request was to go and buy myself one. Four days after we were married, he cheated. The woman called my house at three and four in the morning when he would not answer his beeper. There were no sexual relations between us after we got married and he still stayed out for days at a time. When he would come home at five and six in the morning, he went straight to the guest room where he would talk on the telephone all night while I would be in my bedroom. There would be times when I would wake up in the morning with no way to go to work because my keys and my car would be gone. I caught a cab to work a few times because of it. One day he came home awfully upset and told me that I had ruined his reputation because everyone had found out that he was married.

THE LONG DISTANCE CALL

While opening the phone bill one day, it was so high that I refused to pay it. There were so many unfamiliar long distance telephone numbers on it, but pages and pages of one particular number that was being called every day, several times a day. It was in Ft. Lauderdale, so I called it. Prior to calling, I called Josephine, a church member and friend to be a witness on the telephone because Victor had been telling so many lies about me to his family, my friends, and the church members. Sister Jo, as we called her, was a sister from the church who had been trying to minister to both Victor and me. She had encouraged me greatly and was trying to give both Victor and me words of wisdom, while being impartial. She was a true woman of God who loved the Lord and loved His people. Victor had been playing on her sympathy and telling her how I was mistreating him and how hard he had been working at making the marriage work. He would also tell his family and other people from the church all sorts of twisted stories about me. Moreover, he would tell people that I needed psychological help, told people that I made up stories, and that I had a mental problem. I would say to him: *"You have no job, no car, no place to live, no money, have been evicted your entire life, have never paid a bill, and you say that I have a mental problem?"*

I called the number with Josephine on the phone as a witness. I introduced myself and explained that I was calling to find out whose number this was on my telephone bill. The woman who answered told me that Victor was her boyfriend. She worked at the Division of Motor Vehicles and told me that she had looked up the tag on "his" car. When she questioned him about the name that the tag was under, he told her that he lived with his sister "Mia," and that "his" car was in his sister's name. The woman told me that Victor said he was single and she believed him because he spent his nights with her. I had heard that before and knew it to be true because of course, he was never at home with me. She then said, *"He's here with me right now."* I asked her to put him on the phone. When he picked up the phone, I asked him where he was. He said, *"I'm at a friend's house, why?"* I said, *"because I'm wondering if you are going to be moving in with your friend. I would be more than willing to pack your things."* I asked the young lady to come and get his belongings. Actually, I begged her to come and get his belongings. She claimed that she did not know he was married and that she was going to leave him alone. That was a lie. I later found out that she did know he was married but did not care as long as she could be with him. While speaking with her, she asked me why I did not seem angry or surprised and mentioned how calm I was. I told her that it was because I had been through this with Victor many, many times before, and that she was not the first, second, third, or fourth, and that she would not be the last. I became angry when she told me that she had been to my home. She stated that there were times when she would come and pick him up because his "sister" needed to borrow his car, so she would come and pick him up to spend the night with her. That infuriated me. It was obvious that the man had no respect for me, but to bring a woman to my house was despicable. I had terminated his use of my car, and on those occasions when I made sure that my purse and keys were safely hid, he would tell her that "his sister" had to borrow "his" car, so the woman would come and get him. There were times that I would be taking a shower, and would come out of the bathroom to find my keys and my car gone. I cannot count the number of times that he brought my car back with no gas. Having to hide my purse, my wallet, and my keys in my own home was more than I could bear. Why should I have to hide my purse in my own home?

BUSTED

Just as he had called my mother and others with lies about the stripper, like clockwork, he called Sister Josephine from church the very next day. She had listened on the phone and knew the whole story already, but she allowed him to talk. She admitted that if she had not known the truth for herself, she would have believed every word that he told her. He had a knack for being very charismatic and seemingly sincere, which is how he had so many people fooled. After he finished telling her his well thought-out, fabricated story, she told him that she was on the phone, had heard everything from beginning to end, and knew that he had been committing adultery and lying about everything else. She further told him that what he was doing to me was wrong and that he could not expect to get blessed with the kind of fruit that he was bringing forth. She continued to tell him that she did not appreciate him taking her kindness for weakness when she had only been trying to minister to him. She said that he should be ashamed of himself for all of the things he had done to me and was still doing. Lastly, she told him not to call her anymore. Needless-to-say, he turned on her and made up lies about her to the members in the church. She apologized to me and told me that she had believed all of his lies and that she actually felt sorry for him because she thought that he was really the victim and was being mistreated.

MARRIAGE COUNSELING

The church intervened and tried to help salvage the marriage. Victor lied to the Pastor and the Pastor's wife. He had won them over with his charisma and fabrications and had them thinking that everything was my fault. He would call them without my knowledge and make up all sorts of stories about me just as he had been doing with family and others. However, when the Pastor would ask me about the accusations in Victor's presence, it would be revealed that he was lying. It did not take them long to find out the truth about him. The Pastor became annoyed and asked him one day, *"Why do you lie so much?"* It also did not take the men of the church long to find out about him. But Victor avoided the men. He would approach the women in the church and play on their emotions and sympathy. He did not talk to the men much.

Although the Pastor and his wife knew that Victor did not perform the duties that a man should fulfill as the head of household, they still tried to save the marriage. Victor played with the church and used the Bible when it benefited him. He began quoting scriptures to me such as, *"A wife should submit herself to her husband."* I would come right back with a scripture such as, *"... if any provide not for his own, and especially for those of his own house, he hath denied the faith, and is worse than an infidel"* (1 Tim 5:8). He constantly lied in marriage counseling and as soon as the counseling was over, he would call me all sorts of names and say horrible things to me. He did not care about the marriage at all. He just wanted to stabilize his security. I reciprocated. I was just as bad as him at this point. I was no longer the sweet, kind, mild-mannered person he knew me to be before the baby. I had turned into a monster, who had no respect for him, and would say anything that came to mind, and my words were lethal. He knew my position on marriage, and would often tell people, *"She will never divorce me because she doesn't believe in divorce."* During a counseling session, the Pastor plainly told him to start coming home every night. He said, *"When the sun goes down, you should be at home with your wife."* Victor tried it for six days, but on the seventh day, he had to rest – right in the bed of another woman. He was gone for two days. Had he come home on the seventh day, I would have been able to say that for the first time, my husband spent seven consecutive nights at home, but it never happened.

Both the Pastor and his wife were shocked beyond belief when I told them that Victor had never paid one bill, had never bought me a Christmas gift, birthday present, or Valentines gift. When I told them that we had never been out on a date, never been out to dinner, or seen a movie together, they were flabbergasted. But when I told them that we had never kissed, one could have knocked them over with a feather. The Pastor repeated, *"You have never kissed?"* He had never heard anything like that in his life from a married couple. I tried to convince them that the man did not love me and that he had married me for convenience. They didn't want to believe it, but was finally seeing the truth of the matter after coming into revelation of the things I had been telling them all along. Victor was sitting there the entire time. The Pastor turned to him and said: *"Why did you marry her if you didn't love her"?* His answer was, *"because I do love her"*. I interjected and said, *"Name one thing you ever did to show me that you love me, one thing."* I told them that I knew he didn't love me and I was okay with it. I was at the point that I just wanted a divorce. All that "I don't believe in divorce" stuff was out the window. This man had given me a run for my money, and I was ready to throw in the towel. I thought that after hearing about my horrible marriage, they would have said, *"We think that a divorce would probably be the best thing."* But, they still believed that the marriage could be saved. I guess that I appreciate what they were trying to do, but what they failed to realize was that the marriage was founded upon lies and deceit, not love. It was built upon sinking sand from day one, and there was never any hope for it because there was never a solid foundation on which to build. It was unhealthy from the beginning. A lasting relationship begins a healthy relationship. Many couples who end up in divorce start off being in love. Then, for whatever reasons, the love diminishes, and they grow apart. However, they have memories of the good times they shared and sometimes the good times outweighed the bad. Victor and I never had any good times. We could never say, remember when we were in love, or remember when we used to hold hands and walk on the beach, go out to dinner, watch movies, look at television together, laugh and play together, or talk to each other and share dreams and visions with each other. We never did any of those things, so we had no memories of any good times. There were none. The marriage was built on lies, deceit, manipulation, and quick sinking sand.

During marriage counseling with the Pastors, I had not slept with Victor in almost a year. In an effort to help the marriage, the Pastor recommended that we start dating. He suggested that we watch a rented movie and begin sleeping in the same bed. I became pregnant. That was the first time in a year and also the last time that we were ever together sexually. His antics became excessively worse. The pregnancy was as horrible as the first one. I was constantly left home alone with no way of getting anywhere, because he would take my car and be gone for days.

One morning when I was seven months pregnant, I heard Victor getting up early to leave with the car. There was absolutely no food in the house, so before he left, I told him that I needed to go to the grocery store because there was nothing in the house to eat. That was around 9:10a.m. He told me that he would be back in 20 minutes. He did not return until 11:30pm the next day. I was so hungry and being pregnant made it that much worse. After he hadn't come by the evening, I called the Pastors, and they brought me something to eat. By then, I think they knew that it was effortless to try and salvage the so-called marriage, but they never said anything. I tried to get a divorce while I was pregnant, but no attorney wanted to represent me in my condition. This pregnancy was different from the first one. With Stephanie, I never argued or fussed, never questioned him about anything. I purposely remained calm for the sake of the baby. With this pregnancy, I had gotten so used to yelling and screaming, that I did not have the inner strength to force myself to be calm. It was just a horrible experience and an awful pregnancy.

When the police were called out, they would say that someone had to leave the home for the night. Victor would say, *"I am not leaving because I live here."* I was the one who always had to leave. Twice, I was pregnant when I was made to leave my home because he refused to go. The first time, I was six months pregnant, and the second time, I was eight months pregnant. The second time I left, I drove my car to a park and slept in it all night. This man, knowing that I was pregnant, would agree to make me leave my own home, where I paid every bill. That was the kind of man that I attracted into my life and I had to painfully ask God what was inside of me that could attract something so repulsive? Even the police officers felt sorry for me. Most times, it was the same two officers who came out. One day, as one of them was walking me to my car, he asked me, *"Don't you have a father or any brothers?"* When I answered, "no" to both, he said, *"I wish you were my sister."* Men like Victor love women who have no father or brothers in their lives to protect them. It is so sad.

TIME FOR FREEDOM

When it was time for the baby to be born, that man called me every name in the book on the way to the hospital and would not even stay the night after his son was born. He came back to the hospital two days later when it was time for me to be released. I tried with every fiber in my being to get along with him because I had this newborn baby boy, and I did not want negative energy around him. There was no contending with this man. The day that the baby and I were coming home from the hospital, I asked Victor if he would stop by the store so that I could buy some purified water. He told me that he did not have time to stop because he had somewhere to be (in my car). I told him that I really needed the water and that he needed to stop so that I could get it. An argument ensued. I had totally lost respect for him and I was so disgusted at the fact that he knew I had just had a baby and needed purified water, but his desire to go be with another woman was more important than seeing to it that his wife and child had what they needed. If there was any shred of respect for him, it was totally eradicated after that day.

I finally came to grips with the fact that I had to be the one to move if I was going to get rid of this man because he wasn't going anywhere, and he had made that perfectly clear. It would be a major inconvenience for me because I would be breaking a rental contract. I had also been discussing purchasing the condo with the owner. It was a nice condominium on the lake and had a very nice deck out back, but I had to make the sacrifice of moving for my sanity and peace of mind. I needed to make a move because Victor certainly was not going to. I had a newborn baby, but I could not take anymore of the hell. I thought constantly about how my baby girl had died, and I did not want what happened to her to happen to my son, because I believed deep down inside, that Victor's demonic forces contributed somehow to my daughter's death. I had to protect this little boy at all costs. Therefore, one day, while Victor was on one of his excursions, I called Derrick, a friend of mine, who I had not spoken with in years, but he had always been a good friend to me, and one I knew could be counted on. I told him about Victor and all I had been going through. He rented me a U-Haul, brought some guys with him, and they moved every piece of furniture out of that Condominium. I had already made arrangements to move in with a friend until I could get on my feet, and that is exactly what I did. When I left, I had the electricity and water turned off. The phone had already been disconnected. I was leaving my past behind me. I had finally done what I should have done long before that. I was off to a new and fresh start.

THE TWO BLESSINGS

Finally getting away from that man was the best thing I could have done. When he came home to an empty house, it was three days later. He called my cellular continuously, desperately begging me on the voicemail not to leave him. He begged and cried claiming that he had no place to go. I reminded him that he had boldly told me on many occasions that he had plenty of places to go. I also reminded him that a man who had never slept home must already have an alternate home somewhere. His personal problems were not my concern, and I did not care to hear about his sad story. He continued to call for days, weeks, months and even years. I would look at my caller ID and not answer. When I did answer I would quickly end the conversation. I had finally freed myself, and I was not going to allow him to yoke me up again! My life immediately became better, my head became clearer, I began to gain weight again, and I found myself laughing more. I had peace of mind again. I divorced him eight months after I left him. I purchased my first home a year later and God has blessed me abundantly since.

   As I look back in retrospect, I can clearly see how playing with fire got me severely burnt. I had third degree burns on most of my spiritual body. I allowed the spirit of loneliness to lead me to call a man that I was not compatible with nor equally yoked to, all for the sake of having someone to talk to. I can also now see that it was a setup to destroy me by the enemy from the very beginning. This man was sent to me at Burger King, but I resisted. He was sent again at the grocery store, but I did not resist. I gave in to temptation and paid the price for it dearly. Inasmuch as I judged others for allowing themselves to get into destructive relationships, I was judged. I had blamed and talked about other women until I had to walk in those very same shoes. Unfortunately, I had the devastating and agonizing experience of living the nightmare of every woman's story I had heard. The experience was so awful for me that I had completely lost control of myself. Through my lack of self-control, I had inflicted upon myself far-reaching sufferings of indescribable torment, both of mind and soul. But once I was able to clearly reflect on all that I had gone through, I realized that regardless of what I endured, I was still responsible for my every action and had to regard the wrong actions of Victor as a test of my own strength. All of my weaknesses, sins, hurt, pain, disappointments, and rises and falls, originated in my own heart. I, and only I was responsible for that. Yes, there was and will always be tempters and provokers, but temptations and provocations are powerless to those refusing to respond to them. Once I came to grips with that, I knew that I was on a path that led to wisdom and peace.

Always remember that if you are with someone who brings out the absolute worst in you, that person is definitely not the one for you. You need to be with someone who brings out the best in you, who makes you laugh, who will cry when you cry, but not make you cry; hurt when you hurt, but not deliberately hurt you. If you find yourself changing for the worst and doing and saying things that are uncharacteristic of your personality, remove yourself from that situation quickly. The longer you stay, the worse you will become. Don't waste your time on a person who is not bringing out your best qualities.

I have always heard that every adversity carries with it the seed of tomorrow's victory, and every sadness carries with it the seed of tomorrow's joy. The Lord always leads us to victory if we persevere. If we stay close to Him, we will never fail. Every trial is for the purpose of changing us into His image. Never waste a single trial. If your path is more difficult, it is because of your high calling. Discipline yourself for righteousness. I must admit that the things I went through were devastating for me, but I made it through them. There is always a way over, around, or through. I refuse to grieve over my bad choices and denied gratifications. I will not live in the past and have constant regrets of my bad experiences. I give thanks for the seeds of joy that emanated from such challenges. There were two seeds of joy that came out of those trying times. My two children Stephanie and Stephan. Stephanie is in heaven with God and Stephan is peacefully in his bed asleep as I write this sentence. Perhaps that was the only purpose for me meeting Victor – for him to give me those specific children that no one else in this world could have given to me. Who knows?

~~ LESSONS LEARNED ~~

1. Exercising control over your tongue and actions strengthens and refines your character.

2. We must live with the consequences from the decisions we make, but God always make a way of escape when we are truly ready to be freed of the burden.

3. There is always something good that comes out of every adversity and pain. We must not let the pain blind us from recognizing the good.

~~REFLECTION QUESTIONS ~~

1. How have you dealt with relationships that were burdensome and psychologically draining? Did you let them linger, did you free yourself from them, or are you still in them?

2. What type of people are you attracting into your life? Do they bring out your best qualities?

3. Do you allow your thoughts to control your actions or do you force your actions to control your thoughts?

*C*hapter
6

Live Today as Your Last Day on Earth
Memories Last a Lifetime

*W*hy *have you been allowed to live this extra day
when others far better have departed this earth? Is it because
they have accomplished their purpose in life when yours is still
yet to be achieved? Is this another opportunity for you to become
the person you know you can be?*

*Destroy procrastination with action. Bury doubt with
faith. Dismember fear with confidence. Today is the tomorrow
that you worried about yesterday, and all is well! This moment,
this day, is as good as any moment in all eternity. Make this day,
each moment of this day, a heaven on earth.*

*The duties of today you shall fulfill today. Today you
shall spend time with your children while they are still here.
Tomorrow they will be gone, and so will you. Today you shall
embrace your sweetheart with tender kisses; tomorrow they will
be gone, and so will you. Today you shall lift up a friend in need;
tomorrow they will no longer need your help, nor will you hear
their request. Today you shall give yourself in sacrifice and
work; tomorrow you will have nothing to give, and there will be
nothing to receive.*

Each minute of today will be more fruitful than the hours of yesterday. Your last will be your last, then you will fall to your knees, and give thanks.

WHAT'S WRONG WITH THE BABY?

May 26, 1997 was the day that my baby girl was born. Stephanie was very aware of her surroundings from the day she arrived. It seemed as though she understood everything that was happening around her. It was obvious that she was a special little baby. However, she never seemed to be happy here on this earth. She never slept peacefully, so I would often lay her on top of me. She would seem to be a little more peaceful when I was holding her, but she still would jerk and jump in fear as if something was tormenting her. It tore me up to see my newborn baby like this. I would pray for her, anoint her, and ask God what was wrong. She seemed to have a little peace when she was in my arms, but I could not always hold her. Whenever her father, Victor would come home, she seemed to get worse. At night, she slept in her crib in the nursery, but I would hear her whimper from the baby monitor. I just did not know what was wrong with her.

MOMMY HAS TO GO TO WORK

Two weeks after Stephanie was born, I had to find employment to bring income into the home. I was an unwed mother with zero financial support from her father. He did not have a job, did not try to find one when I became pregnant, and still did not have one after she was born, so I had to go to work. I secured a temporary job after just having had a baby two weeks prior. Stephanie was born in May and since school was out in June, the summer should have given me time to recuperate and establish a bond with my newborn, but unfortunately, I had to work to keep a roof over our heads.

SICK ON THE JOB

It was time for school to start again, and as a teacher, I had to report back to work two days prior to the students. Unfortunately, I had caught a bad cold a few days prior to returning back, so on my first day, I felt awful. I woke up late and did not have time to dress the baby, so I asked Victor to do it for me. As we were leaving the house, I remember looking at Stephanie in her cute little white outfit and thinking that she was so adorable. This would be her first day with her new Hispanic caregiver. Being born and raised in Miami-Dade County, I knew that the benefits of being bilingual were great, and I wanted Stephanie to be bilingual. Her new caregiver came highly recommended by my mother's neighbor, and when I interviewed the lady, I was very impressed. She had a sweet and loving spirit and an immaculate home with a designated area for the babies she cared for. She had three others babies, and individual cribs for each of them. I felt very comfortable with leaving Stephanie in her care.

So here I was being dropped off to work, feeling sick with the Flu and running late. As Stephanie's dad drops me off, he says, *"Aren't you going to kiss the baby?"* I said, *"I want to, but I don't want to be in her face with this bad cold. I'll see her later."* Well, the next time I would kiss Stephanie would be hours later, after her death.

While at work, I felt awful. I had no energy, a sinus headache, and my nose was stuffed up. All I wanted to do was go home. I told my boss how I was feeling and she told me that I could leave. I called Stephanie's father who had my car and asked him to pick me up. It was about 12:00 noon at that time. I was ready to collapse by then. I just wanted to sleep, and I expressed that to him, but he insisted that we pick the baby up right then. That way, he could drop us both off and not come home until the next morning when it was time for me to go to work as he usually did. I, on the other hand was thinking that since the baby had to be picked up before 5:00 p.m., I could go home, take some medicine, get some rest and then pick her up when I felt a little better before 5:00 p.m. After a heated argument, I managed to get him to take me home before picking Stephanie up. I do not think there was ever a time that Stephanie's father made any sense, and even though he did not make sense that day, perhaps I should have picked her up, because she was still alive at the very time I left work.

On the way home, I stopped and bought some Flu medicine. When I arrived home, I took the medicine, took the phone off the hook, and climbed into bed. I woke up around 3:00 p.m. and put the phone back on the hook. Stephanie's dad had left me a message saying that he did not think he would be able to pick her up before 5:00 p.m., and could I find someone else to get her. I called my mother and asked her if she could pick the baby up for me. She agreed. In the meantime, I forgot to turn the telephone ringer back on and I missed all calls after that.

THE TELEPHONE MESSAGES

About 45 minutes later, I realized that the ringer was still off, so I turned it back on and there were many new messages. The first one was from Stephanie's dad saying that he in fact was going to pick her up, and was on his way. When I picked up the second message, it was my mother saying, *"Mia, I am here at the baby sitter's house and there are police officers here and yellow tape everywhere. The baby is not here. They say that she had problems breathing, and she is at Parkway Hospital."* I frantically fell down on my knees and prayed that she was okay. At that moment, all I could think about was how tormented she always seemed to be. I just wanted to pick her up and hold her in my arms. I ran outside to find anyone in a car to ask him or her for a ride to the hospital. I did not see anyone. I went back inside and called my cousin, Keith who came immediately, although it seemed like an eternity.

WHERE IS MY BABY?

When I arrived at the hospital, everyone seemed to know who I was. When I asked the security guard where the children's ward was, he said *"Are you Mrs. Sanders?"* and he showed me where to go. As I entered, I asked the nurses at the station, *"Where is my baby?"* they said, *"Are you Mrs. Sanders?"* They contacted someone on the phone and immediately a female doctor came out to talk to me. I kept asking, *"Where is my baby? Where is my baby?"* She said, *"I need to ask you a couple of questions first."* She asked if the baby had been sick, if there were any unusual problems with her lately, had I noticed anything different about her. The answer to each question was, *"No, where is my baby?"* I finally said, *"Is my baby all right?"* The doctor said, *"No, it's serious".* She took me into a conference room where I saw my mother, Stephanie's father, medical personnel, and police detectives. My mother's eyes were bloodshot red and Stephanie's father was crying. I asked the question one last time, *"Where is my baby?"* The next five words that came out of that doctor's mouth pierced my soul like a sharp sword. She said, *"Your baby was found expired."* All I remember was me screaming to the top of my lungs. The baby had died at the baby sitter's house around 2:30p.m. I was at home sleeping. No one called me until 4:45p.m., rather no one left a message until that time. All of my numbers where in the baby's bag. Stephanie's father and my mother had arrived at the sitter's house at the same time. They both left and headed straight to the hospital. No one came by the house to get me. The baby was dead.

The medical examiner determined Sudden Infant Death Syndrome (SIDS) to be the cause of death. Stephanie was buried Wednesday of the next week. I felt an overwhelming sense of grief and guilt. I felt as though I should have picked her up from the sitter when I left work that day. I should have spent more time with her. I should have been the one to dress her that morning. I should have kissed her when I got out of the car that morning. Maybe she felt like I didn't want her since I was almost never there for her because I was working all of the time. Finally, I had to come to grips with the reality that she was never happy on this earth and she was going to leave anyway. As I look back on everything in retrospect, it was better that she died while I wasn't around because I would have been a basket case had she done it at home while I was in the house. I thank God that it happened the way it did because it also removes doubt from others that I contributed in any way to her death. I know how some people think when babies die at home with the parents in the house. What if we would have picked her up when I left work and she died while I was in the bed asleep? Imagine how I would have felt awakening to find my child dead in her crib. God knew what he was doing. He makes no mistakes.

THE 93-DAY VISIT

I am thankful that I had the opportunity to have Stephanie for 93 days. I often still thank God for her. I can't help but wonder why she had to die. What was making her so frightened here? Why did she have to come and go so abruptly? I needed to be in the presence of the Lord right away, so the day she died, I came home from the hospital, lifted my hands to God, and began to Praise and Worship Him. Every pain we suffer brings us closer to divine wisdom and brings us closer to God. My heart was shattered into pieces, but I needed to praise him to keep my sanity. Do you have a better understanding of why it is so important to live each day as if it were your last? If I had the chance to repeat that day, all of my actions would have been different. It was a long road ahead for me, and I am still healing. Stephanie would have been ten years old on May 26, 2007. May she be at peace now, and may God bless her little soul.

PRECIOUS MOMENTS

My grandfather died on June 14, 2002. His body was consumed with cancer, but his mind was sharp and still full of wisdom. Although he wasn't my biological grandfather, he always treated me as if I was one of his own. He called me every year on my birthday until he became ill. I did not spend as much time with him as I would have liked to, but I still spent some time in his presence before he died. I had an opportunity to talk to him and ask him questions about his life. He shared some of his life's experiences as well as some of his youthful indiscretions with me and I enjoyed our little talks. They made me feel good. Prior to his death, he asked to see all of his grandchildren and great-grandchildren. He knew that his days were numbered, and he was ready. He was eighty-two years old, and would often tell people that God had blessed him with three-score and two years. He shared with me that he had no regrets, and that he had lived a full life with a faithful and loving wife. He had cancer, but endured absolutely no pain. The doctors were astounded and could not understand how he experienced no pain. We can still be blessed in the midst of infirmities. On the day he died, I called to check on him, and my grandmother told me that he had died about an hour before my call. Initially I cried, but then I wiped the tears from my eyes and rejoiced

107

because I knew he was spiritually ready to go. He had said at some point before he passed that he had seen a white cloud and that he was ready to step on to it. Had I not been to see him, I would have felt extremely sad and guilty. We must live today as our last day on earth.

IN PERSPECTIVE

As humans, we take so much for granted. We oftentimes don't show appreciation for the small, yet important things that bring meaning to our lives. We love to place emphasis on things with an expensive price tag and yet place little emphasis on things that are free. We value big houses, luxurious cars, designer clothes, expensive jewelry, name-brand purses, boats, yachts, etc. Living the American Dream in the good ole USA has gotten us caught up in materialism. Houses, cars, clothes, jewelry, and boats can all perish in a matter of seconds and yet can all be replaced. However, when a life is gone, that life can never be replaced, yet we seem to place little value on human life. We should highly value the free gifts: our health and strength, family and friends, knowledge and awareness, and our thoughts, because when those *free* gifts are gone, they are gone forever. You cannot put a price tag on those things. They can never be replaced.

Unfortunately, many of us do not have that revelation yet because we are still trying to be like, and keep up with the Jones'. Sometimes it takes a tragic situation to have our perspectives put in proper order. If you talk to a suffering cancer patient who was once strong and vivacious and lived an abundant life, they will tell you how very insignificant materials things seem in comparison to their deteriorating health. They will tell you that none of their material things meant a hill of beans because without health, they can't enjoy them. Priorities immediately change when a terminal diagnosis is given. Talk to a person who has endured a life-threatening illness, but has been blessed to overcome that sickness, and is still living. I guarantee you that person will tell you once they realized there was a possibility that they could depart earth in the very near future, their entire perception about life changed. Material things shrunk to their proper sizes and each day became a gift. Their children became precious in their eyes and each day they were able to behold them as such. The things that they would previously get upset about were then petty and insignificant in retrospect. The things that created wedges between them and other people had also seemed petty and foolish as they realized how much time had been wasted. They began to live each day as if it were their last. There is nothing that can humble a person faster than to lose all physical mobility and have to have others care for them. Sense of independence is gone and dignity is significantly diminished. Tomorrow is promised to nobody and we never know when we shall breathe our last breath. That is why we should greet each day with love in our heart and live today as our last day on earth.

FORGIVENESS

Healthy married couples argue occasionally, which is normal. But let's say that you had a terrible argument with your spouse who you love dearly. You said some horrible things and without apologizing, you both go off to work. What if you are the only one who returns home, but your spouse was killed in a car accident on their way home from work? Can you imagine the overwhelming guilt that you would feel for not having attempted to apologize for the argument? How long do you think that guilt would last? It would take some serious healing through prayer to get over that because you would first have to forgive yourself.

One problem with many of us is that we are still beating

109

ourselves up over something that God forgave us for a long time ago. When we cannot forgive ourselves, we certainly cannot forgive others. Had you put into practice the love and forgiveness that we are called to extend towards one another, you would have attempted to apologize before you both went off to work. That is the true test of character, when you have a justifiable reason to get upset over an offense, but you force yourself into reciprocating with love. It is not easy, but there is a powerful force that crushes the head of the enemy when good is chosen over evil. Even if the apology was not accepted right away, at least you would have tried. In that manner, your spouse would have known that you were truly sorry, and that you still love them in spite of the argument. Your grief would not have been compounded by the guilt, from you not apologizing.

Too many people let others leave this earth without making amends and telling them how they feel. Unfortunately, when the person dies, there is tremendous guilt and grief. We must swallow our pride and make peace with whom we need to make peace and only you know who those people are. When it comes to forgiveness, it does not matter whose fault it was. You are the bigger person who is striving to be like Christ, so *you* apologize. Apologies should not consist of "if... thens." "*If* I have done something to hurt or wrong you, *then* I'm sorry". That's not a genuine apology. A genuine apology sounds something like this: *"I am sorry for hurting you, I am sorry for mistreating you. I am sorry for... I was wrong, and I hope that you forgive me."* No buts after the apology, just *I am sorry for...* period! You have now taken responsibility for your actions, and even if the other person wronged you, forgive them, and tell them that you have forgiven them, sincerely. There would be no need to get into details; all that does is open old wounds. Apologize and go forward from there. You will feel a heavy load being lifted off of your shoulders. If your apology is not going to be sincere, then do not even bother. You are not ready yet. But remember, time waits for no one. Live today as your last day on earth.

~~ **LESSONS LEARNED** ~~

1. Time waits for no one. Sometimes we have to make small sacrifices of time to spend with loved ones in order to make precious memories. Tomorrow is not promised. A person may be here today and gone tomorrow. Make the most of each day.

2. We often think that things should have been different, but God knows the end from the beginning and everything is played out just the way He has planned it.

~~**REFLECTION QUESTIONS**~~

1. Are you taking the time to visit family members and friends to make those precious memories that mean so much to others and yourself?

2. When is the last time you sat at the feet of an elderly person and just listened to them talk to you about whatever it is they want to talk about?

*C*hapter

7

Believe That You are a Miracle
Complete in Christ

*G*od *danced the day you were born! Since the
beginning of time there has never been another with your mind,
your heart, your eyes, your ears, your hands, your hair, your
mouth. No one who came before, no one who lives today, and
no one who comes tomorrow will walk and talk and move
exactly like you! You are rare, and there is value in rarity,
therefore you are valuable!*

*Don't look for miracles because you are a miracle. Don't
compare yourself with others because you are a unique and
beautiful creation.*
*Don't let yesterday's accomplishments be sufficient for
today's commitments, nor should you indulge anymore in self-
praise for deeds, which in reality are too small to even
acknowledge.*

*You are here for a purpose and that purpose is to grow
into a mountain, not to shrink to a grain of sand. Henceforth,
you will apply all your efforts to become the highest mountain of
all, and you will strain your potential until it cries for mercy!*

*Seek constantly to improve your manners and graces, for
they are the sugar to which all are attracted.*

Your problems, discouragements and heartaches are really great opportunities in disguise. You should no longer be fooled by the natural garments they wear because your eyes are open wide. Look beyond the natural and do not be deceived.

THE SUPERNATURAL FALL

When I reflect over my life, I thank the Lord for how far He has brought me. My self-destructive behaviors were leading me down a path of failure, misery, destruction and death. I could have been dead in my grave had it not been for the Lord who has kept me. At a very young age, my life started down the wrong path, but because somebody had prayed for me, the hand of God and the mercy of God were with me.

When I look at my son, I can't help but praise the Lord because I count occasions when the forces of evil tried to take his life. Two stand out vividly in my mind. As I write this chapter, my heart is filled with gratitude because the memories of how the hand of God was upon my child flood my mind. When my son was nine months old, we were temporarily living with a friend because I had left my husband and was in the process of getting a divorce. She had a room that she had converted into a small office where her computer was located. Also in the room was a futon that sat very high. This particular day, I was using her computer while my son lie asleep on the futon behind me. Something made me turn around to check on the baby, and as I turned, all I could see was my baby falling on the floor very fast – head first. Since he had already begun falling, I knew that I could not get to him in time to catch him. All I could think about was the hard tile floor and my baby's head hitting it. All of a sudden, as the baby was falling, he began to move in slow motion. It was as though some unseen entity had come and placed its wings under my child's body and then gently laid him on the floor. The child had awakened without me hearing a sound and he was about to crack his head open on that floor, but a supernatural intervention happened, and I witnessed it! My baby was gently placed on the floor, and he began laughing excitedly. When I saw that, I began praising and worshiping God right then and there. The scripture in Psalm 91 where it says ... *for he will give his angels charge over thee, to keep thee in all the ways. They shall bear thee up in their hands...* became alive and real in my life at that very moment. The angels held my son in their hands. I will never forget that day, and as I write, the tears flow down my face because of how God protected and covered my son. I think that through that experience, God was telling me that he was not going to allow me to go through the pain that I endured with the loss of Stephanie. I think that deep down inside, I was afraid that I would lose my son prematurely as I had lost my daughter. After this experience however, I knew that God was protecting my child and all fears of him being taken away were erased from that day on. My child is a miracle, and God is keeping him here for His divine purpose.

THE LITTLE CLIMBER

After my divorce from Victor, the Lord blessed us with our first home. My son and I had our own house. It was a modest two bedroom, two bathroom home in a quiet neighborhood. I was blessed to be able to furnish every room in the house - my bedroom, my son's bedroom, and the living room, in a relatively short period of time. It was such a gratifying feeling to have purchased something that I could call my own. It was so peaceful coming home everyday and being happy. Stephan was almost two years old, in school, talking way too much, and was a happy little boy. One Thursday evening after he and I had come home, I asked him to get his pajamas out of his drawer in preparation for his bath. About 30 seconds later after he ran into his room, I heard loud crashing noises. I ran from the kitchen into his bedroom and the sight of what I saw caused me to panic. I saw his furniture chest on top of his little body and the huge 19" television that was sitting on top of the chest was on top of his head! I felt the energy leaving my body and I knew that I was about to faint, but as I got closer, I saw that the child had not been touched by neither the chest nor the television. I noticed that the edge of the bed had stopped the chest from falling directly on top of his body and the television was brought to a standstill at the edge of the bed where his head was. I could see how the chest was stopped by the bed, but there was nothing to be seen by the natural eye to explain how the TV was hanging *over* the child's head. Immediately, I lifted the heavy television and placed it on the floor. It appeared as though time had been frozen to where the chest and the TV could not complete their falls. Stephan was between them both lying on the bed with the chest at his feet and the television at his head. When I had asked him to get his clothes, he had a tendency to climb on the knobs of the chest to the top drawer where his underclothes were kept in order to reach them. In doing this on this day, it caused the television and the chest to both slide forward, knocking him onto the bed. What a miracle that he was not killed! If that chest did not crush him, the television definitely would have. Again, in looking at the positions of the objects, something unseen had to have been holding them in their places until I arrived. Needless-to-say, his underwear/pajama drawer is now at the bottom of the chest, so no climbing is necessary. My child is a miracle indeed. To God be the glory!

A BUCK 05

We live in a country where we initially accept or reject others based on their outward appearance. Physical appearances seem to take precedence over many things these days, including competence and skills. Much pressure is placed on beauty and weight that peer pressure among teenagers and adolescents to look like Barbie Dolls and Calvin Klein models is very prevalent. Many people are unhappy with some part of their physical appearance, and as a result of their dissatisfaction, they modify areas of their body in an effort to look better, feel better, and be accepted. People typically complain that they are overweight, underweight, too short, etc. I know from experience what that is like because for years I was totally dissatisfied with being so very thin. I hated being skinny. From the age of 19 to the age of 30, I tried gaining weight while everyone else was striving to lose weight. I took all kinds of weight-gaining pills, shakes, SSS Tonic, and many other things in an effort to put on pounds. Of course, people would tell me that my weight was just fine and that I needed not to gain a pound, but when I looked into the mirror, all I could see was skin and bones. It never did take much food to fill me up, so no matter how much I would eat, I just could not gain weight. Regardless of what anyone told me, I was still self-conscience about this, and it lowered my self-esteem. After my breakup with Robert, I lost even more weight. I stayed home as much as I could. I hated seeing anyone I knew because I was embarrassed that I was so skinny.

I went to the daycare to pick up my Goddaughter one day and I ran into someone I knew from high school. We were fairly good friends, so I really expected a pleasant greeting from her. Instead of greeting me happily, she said, *"Isn't your name Mia?"* I said, *"Yes, and your name is Shauntelle."* She then said, *"What happened to you, you are so skinny?"* We did not hug and there were no pleasantries exchanged. She had a repulsive look on her face as if I had a contagious, infectious disease. I was hurt because we were very close in high school and she used to call me her big sister. One would have thought that we were die-hard enemies after that encounter. I went home and cried like a baby. After that, I remained secluded in my apartment with the exception of going back and forth to work and places I absolutely had to go. I know first hand what it is like to be unhappy with one's appearance.

LOOKING PAST APPEARANCE

Ideally, we should be content with our appearance because God, in His wisdom, purpose, and creativity has made us each unique. In fact, His word says that we are "fearfully and wonderfully made" (Psalm 139:14). Our life and all it entails is not about physical appearance, because our spirit is so much deeper than mere looks. Our physical bodies are only shells that hold our spirit and the spirit of a person is what makes him or her who he or she is. That is what it is really about, the spirit of a person, what is deep inside the heart. There are beautiful spirits in this world, and if we took the time to look past the physical appearance, we would discover the most precious people in the world.

When God looks at us, He looks beyond the appearance and directly into the heart. When Isaiah prophesized about the coming of Jesus, he said in Isaiah 53:2 *"...and when we shall see him, there is no beauty that we should desire him."* Jesus was rejected because He *looked* like an ordinary man. There was no majestic or powerful supremacy emanating from His person. He was not wearing the finest of garments, nor did He come wearing a crown of gold. Jesus Christ suffered the ultimate rejection. He was jeered, spat on, threatened, and finally put to death. Everywhere He went, He faced rejection. But man's view of Him never altered His focus. If the people knew God, they would have recognized Jesus by the spirit of God that was in Him. We judge the outer appearance way too much and often make critical, life-changing mistakes because of our superficial judgments.

I am not saying that appearance does not matter. Your appearance does matter, and we should strive to look our best at all times because our appearance is the first basis for evaluation that other people have. People look at us, make a quick and often subconscious judgment, and then treat us accordingly. But most importantly, we should strive to display those precious attributes that have nothing to do with outer appearance. These qualities can never be purchased with silver or gold. Love, humility, wisdom, integrity, compassion, understanding, and purity are but a few. Coincidentally, when we display that kind of fruit, our outer appearance is reflected and the glory of God makes us beautiful. Do you want to be attractive? Put on the garments of praise, humility, grace, excellence, love, joy, peace, patience, kindness, goodness, faithfulness, gentleness, and self-control. As we begin to walk with God, we begin to walk in His nature.

ACCEPTING YOURSELF

Yes, you are a miracle, which is why you are *"fearfully and wonderfully made" (Psalm 139:14)*. You are valuable in God's sight and He loves you deeply and cares about every aspect of your life. There is a reason that you have the personality that you do, the abilities that you do, the aspirations that you do. There is a reason that you are different from everybody else. He made you different for His own purpose. One of my favorite quotes written by Marianne Williamson is the following: *"A tulip doesn't strive to impress anyone. It doesn't struggle to be different than a rose. It doesn't have to. It is different. And there's room in the garden for every flower."*

    If you are not content with the person that God has made you to be, inside and out, then you will never truly be content or able to accept anyone else and their flaws. Why? because you do not truly love yourself and all that you are. We see in others what we see in ourselves. Until you are able to accept who you are, how you look, and how God has created you to be, you will always find fault in others. T.D. Jakes wrote in his book, The Lady, Her Lover, and Her Lord, that *"when we don't value ourselves, we tend to attract people who support that devalued image."* Respect and love yourself. Have a healthy love and respect for who you are, and when you do, you will be able to love others for who they are and all that God created them to be. Self-approval is essential to healthy living. It is the catalyst from which your goals are emanated, pursued, and accomplished. Self-hatred, guilt, shame, and unforgiveness block your growth. It is time for us to forgive ourselves and move on. Practice loving yourself, pampering yourself, and forgiving yourself. Watch how that new self-perception will carry over into your relationships, your job, and ultimately the world around you. By loving yourself, you open up the possibility for others to love you too. Having confidence in yourself and all that you are is not being arrogant. It is being self-assured and it is very necessary in order to have healthy relationships with others. Walk in this world with humility and grace, yet be confident and fearless!

    Do not be fooled into believing that when you find someone to truly accept and love you, then you will be complete. You will never find that person because he or she does not exist. Until you love, understand, and accept yourself for who you truly are, you will always pursue external relationships with hopes of finding love and acceptance from other people. Find that love and acceptance inside of you. If you don't, your relationships will not last because of the weight that you are putting on another person to give you those things that you should find within yourself. It becomes too much for anyone else to bear, and it's not fair to the other person. You are not an incomplete person looking for someone to complete you. You are already whole and complete in God. What complete man wants an incomplete woman? Even the incomplete man wants a complete woman. There is no void that God can't fill to make you whole again.

DEVELOP SELF-CONFIDENCE

People with self-confidence are inner-directed and self-assured. Their validation is not a function of people liking them or treating them well. They are validated from within. One of the most dominating fears afflicting humans is the fear of rejection. This fear compels one to become the person he or she believes will be accepted or recognized, which will vary from some degree with each new group or situation. A person with self-esteem issues is always looking for acceptance from others. These individuals are looking for others to validate who they are. These people are affected by the way others treat them. If people treat them well, they feel well. If they are not treated well, they become hurt and sometimes depressed, pondering over and over in their minds what they could have done that caused that person not to like them. Their sense of worth comes from other people liking and accepting them. When we get a complete revelation of who we are to God and in God, there will be no need for validation from others because inner strength and tenacity will emerge from confidence in God. As long as God approves of you, that is the only validation you need.

121

Life's experiences are the reason that many suffer with low self-esteem and low self-confidence. Things that have happened to them as children, things too shameful and embarrassing to mention, leave many feeling as if they deserve whatever comes their way and nothing better. They feel undeserving of success, and it is not unusual for such people to unconsciously set about sabotaging their own success. As a result, people use them and abuse them. If you are carrying the weight of a negative experience that has happened in your past, you may be hindering your ability to live fully in the now. Hurtful memories can impede your personal and spiritual growth. It is okay to remember those painful memories in your life in order to make you stronger, but you must control them. If you view all the things that have happened to you, both good and bad, as sources from which to draw strength, you will think and live a higher level of consciousness. Do not let them control you any longer. In his book, The Lady, Her Lover, and Her Lord, T.D. Jakes writes: *"There are some things that can happen to you that leave you disfigured. I do not mean outwardly, but inwardly. Many women in this country are bowed down under the weight and pressure that comes from deep, dark secrets and traumas that have left them twisted and misfigured. Issues, relationships, and incidents leap out of their past and hold them hostage, forever chained to emotional pain."* This is the reason why many do not step out on faith and let their gifts come into fruition. They, meaning men and women, are too haunted by things they want to forget, but just can't seem to.

FINDING FULFILLMENT

Many, many people in this world are living their lives unfulfilled. The enemy of our faith wants us to step out before the appointed time or not move in time, or be in the wrong place at the wrong time, so that we will miss our calling and be unfulfilled. There is nothing more frustrating in life than being unfulfilled in your purpose. God has individually given each of us a purpose. Before you were born, He wrote in the Lambs Book of Life what your assignment was to be on earth. Many people think that after they give their life to the Lord, their purpose is to preach. They feel that if they are not preaching or pastoring, then they are not accomplishing their purpose. That is why so many people are preachers today, even though they have not been called to do so. Your purpose in this life is in direct proportion with the gifts that God has placed inside of you. It could be something that you view as insignificant. We tend to call things insignificant if those things are not glamorous or in the limelight. Your gifts may be sewing clothes or crocheting blankets. It could be that you are a skilled mechanic or plasterer. You may not be able to sing, but maybe you can dance. You may be a creative writer or a meticulous and quality painter or carpenter. Some people can play an instrument by ear and do not even know how to read music. You could be brilliant with numbers, excellent with encouraging other people, an outstanding singer, or a first-rate cook. You may have a gift for cleaning, building things, or writing poetry. God has given each of us at least one gift to be used for His glory. God seeks expression through us each and every day, every hour, every minute, every second, and He expresses Himself through men, women, and children. The variation of gifts we have are all for God. He wants mouths to sing beautiful songs for Him and to speak His truths. He wants hands to play harmonious music for Him, to draw beautiful pictures for Him and to build magnificent skyscrapers for Him. He wants eyes to behold his beauties and to experience His miracles. He wants to express Himself through us because it is him that enjoys all these things. Most of us have many gifts, but we all have at least one. The key is to take your particular talent to a level where it has never been taken before. With the gifts you have been given comes the responsibility to use and develop them. Keep your effort on the areas where you shine. Some of the things other people find boring will actually energize and enrich you if its your gift.

God even gave Adam, who was in the garden of utopia, a purpose. Adam had to rule and subdue. He had to take charge of the garden and be a dresser for it. He had to name each of the animals and keep order. Adam was a perfect man, but he too had to have a purpose. God's purpose for our lives is larger than our plans, goals, or desires. *"Eye hath not seen, nor ear heard, neither have entered into the heart of man, the things which God hath prepared for them that love Him. But God hath revealed them unto us by His Spirit ."* (1 Corin 2:9-10).

I know that you have seen men (and even women) who hang out at the corner store drinking beer all day talking trash and doing nothing productive. They have lost their identity, and are living unfulfilled lives. No one is here by accident. You are not here by chance. God gave you an assignment to complete while on this earth. There is something that you are to do that no one else in this world can do. Even if your mother tried to abort you, the fact that you are here means that you have purpose. There is a reason why you can eat, drink, see, and hear. Develop a sense of urgency in your life and commit yourself to walking in your purpose. Many know what their gifts are, and in knowing what your gifts are, you can sometimes easily find your purpose because your gifts and your purpose coincide with each other. For instance, I know beyond a shadow of a doubt that God gave me the gift of teaching. I love teaching! I am good at it, and when I do it, I am in line with what my purpose on this earth is. I teach children. I teach young adults in Sunday School. I teach college students at the University, I teach when I give presentations and workshops to organizations and corporations. I was sent here to teach. Now, I believe that there are so many other gifts inside of me that have yet to be discovered, but at least I know that when I teach, I am on the path that God has destined for me. My destiny unfolds and expands when I teach. Only through God, can we know all that we are.

The enemy of God and man does not want us fulfilled. Satan even wanted Jesus to be unfulfilled. He wanted him to abort the Calvary, the Golgotha experience. He wanted Jesus to fall down before His appointed time. He told Jesus to jump off the apex and even quoted scripture to Him in an effort to persuade Jesus: *"And saith unto him, if thou be the Son of God, cast thyself down: for it is written, He shall give His angels charge concerning thee, and in their hands they shall bear thee up, lest at any time thou dash thy foot against a stone."* (Mathew 4:6). He tempted our Lord, the Emmanuel, the Prince of Peace, the maker and creator of heaven and earth. The devil tempted Him! Jesus' main mission on earth was to die an agonizing death for our sins. *"For this cause he came into the world and for this cause, He died."* (Mathew 26:53). Jesus knew His purpose and the devil knew that if Jesus had thrown Himself over that pinnacle, he would have caused Him to abort His calling. That is what the forces of evil wants for you too. He wants you to abort your calling, deviate from your purpose, be unfulfilled, and wander to and fro, aimlessly, seeking for things and situations that do not belong to you. When you strive for positions and things that do not rightfully belong to you, there is failure and dissatisfaction. When a person can truly say, *"I desire only that which God desires for me"* (Florence Shinn), all false desires fade out of the mind and a new set of desires is given by the Lord Himself. The enemy of your faith does not want you to be fulfilled.

What is fulfillment? Well, I will first tell you what fulfillment is not. It is not earning a lot of money, achieving materialistic things, being around elite people, achieving certain goals, holding a powerful position or obtaining various degrees. Many people have attained all those things, but are still not fulfilled. Some have earned two and three Ph.D degrees and are still not fulfilled. Some are currently working on a fourth or fifth degree in search of the "feeling" of fulfillment, still trying to fill a void. Do they think that earning degrees will give them the fulfillment they are searching for? The answer is "no."

Fulfillment is not found in degrees, wealth, worldly success, pleasure, family and friends, good teachers, or even reading scripture. Fulfillment is found in righteousness. The person who finds refuge in true righteousness (not self-righteousness), has a wise understanding and a loving heart, and is already fulfilled. He or she is contented and stable whether in success or failure, wealth or poverty, with friends or without friends, educated or uneducated, or in health or sickness. Fulfillment is found in the will of God. It is found in the Word of God. Fulfillment is walking on the path that God has preordained for your life before you were born. It is found when you work on the assignment that God gave to you while you were still in your mother's womb. When you take the time to pray, read the Word of God, and establish a close, genuine relationship with God, He will keep you on the path that leads to fulfillment. It will be revealed to you why you are here. You do not have to search for it. It will come to you. What you seek, is also seeking you.

THE GREATNESS WITHIN YOU

You showed up on this planet with a seed of greatness inside you! When you were born, your possibilities were endless!

There is greatness in all of us, but until you find your purpose and let the gifts that God has placed inside of you flourish, you will never be great. The only way to live a rewarding and fulfilling life, is to spend time with God in prayer. You cannot be fulfilled without accomplishing what God has ordained for your life. Winston Churchill said, "To each there comes in his or her lifetime a special moment when they are tapped on the shoulder and offered the chance to do a very special thing, unique to them and fitted to their talent. What a tragedy if that moment finds them unprepared or unqualified for that which could have been their finest hour." The more you pray, the clearer His will for your life will become. Until then, you will have a void and will constantly search for that feeling of contentment, fulfillment, and the peace that passes all understanding that only God can give. One of my favorite motivational speakers is the inspirational Les Brown. He is the epitome of how having a strong will to be great, a motivation to be successful, a desire to overcome other people's negative predictions, and a strong unwavering faith in God, will bring you to the point of surmounting even your highest expectations. In his book, Live Your Dreams, Les Brown quotes, as it relates to gifts and talents, the following: "*Most people never nurture their gifts, skills and abilities. Each of us has a unique offering. No one else is going to produce your product, write your book, open your academy. And if you don't bring your gift forward, if you die with it inside of you, then we will all suffer from being deprived of your particular genius.*" He further writes, later on in the chapter the following: ...*the richest place on the planet is not some diamond mine or an oil field. It is a cemetery, because in the cemetery, we bury the inventions that were never produced, the ideas and dreams that never became reality, the hopes and aspirations that were never acted upon.* How sad. Most people die never having shared their gifts with the world, thus never being fulfilled. Do you remember the Bible parable of the talents? God gave each man a different amount of talents, and all but one came back with more talents than he gave them. But, the one who was given only one talent, did absolutely nothing with that talent. In fact, he hid it, and when the master came back looking for his profit, the wicked servant had no profit for him. When you don't use the talent that God has given you, you are called wicked. Can you imagine having to face your Lord on judgment day, and He says to you, *"You did not use any of the talents that I gave to you to bless others."* And you say, *"But master, what talents? I did not know that I had talents in me, please show me."* And the Lord shows you the many books that you were supposed to write, the songs that you were supposed to sing, the poems that you were to publish, the businesses that you were to establish, the inventions that you were to create, the people that you were to help, etc. Wouldn't that be a sad situation? You have a unique message to deliver, a unique song to sing, a unique act of love to bestow. This message, this song, and this act of love have been entrusted exclusively to the one and only – you! Don't let your dreams die within you rather than letting them blossom in your lifetime. When I read Les Brown's book, and reached the part where he said, *"No one else is going to write your book,"* something inside of me propelled me to get this book that I had already begun to write and do what was necessary to get it published, because no one else can tell *my* story and I do not want my contribution to the world to die inside of me. The feeling of completion, accomplishment, and gratification will not emerge until you complete that, which you and only you are required to do. Thank you Mr. Brown, for that push. There is nothing worse than starting multiple tasks and not finishing any of them. When you start things and never finish them, you are operating in a spirit of incompletion and failure. Your subconscious gets into the habit of not completing. Remember Chapter 2; Work in a Spirit of

Excellence? Not many things indifferently, but one thing supremely, is the demand of our world. If you scatter your efforts, you cannot expect to succeed. As the within, so the without. I was committed to writing and completing this book the second time around.

KNOW YOUR PLACE

Are you in your right place? Ponder on this for a moment: Think about what it is that you do for a living? Is it in line with what you think your purpose is? Is there fulfillment for you at the end of the day? You may be very busy, but busy doing what? Do you like what you do or do you think that there is something else out there that you ought to be doing? Are you in the right place for God to bless you? Dr. Martin Luther King, Jr. knew his place. When it was time for him to die, he said, *"I'm not worried about anything. I'm not fearing any man. Mine eyes have seen the glory of the coming of the Lord."* He knew why he was here. He knew that he was here to bring liberty in the 1960s. He came here to sing, "We shall overcome." Many think that he died before his time, but in the time that God gave him, he did what he was sent here to do. He was able to close his eyes and rest in peace because his assignment was completed. His life, all that he did with his life showed that he was indeed a miracle. When it is time for you to close your eyes and go to your final resting place, will your assignment be completed? Find your purpose so that you may live a fulfilled life. Spend time with God so that He will guide you and keep you on the path that leads to the unfolding of your destiny. You are a miracle, so start acting like it!

~~ LESSONS LEARNED ~~

1. When we begin to truly love ourselves and everything about us, self-confidence will emerge, and we will develop the wherewithal to accomplish every goal that we set for ourselves.

2. Until we find our purpose and begin walking on the path that God has pre-ordained for us, there will never be fulfillment in our lives. There will always be a void.

3. The seed of greatness is within you. You must cultivate and nurture that seed in order for it to blossom in the earth and bring forth fruit.

~~ REFLECTION QUESTIONS ~~

1. Are you validated from within or do you place emphasis on outer appearances instead of feeding your spirit?

2. Have you identified your purpose on this earth? Are you living a fulfilled life?

3. What have you done to bring out the greatness that is within you? Are you nurturing the gifts that God has placed inside of you?

Chapter

8

Plan for Prosperity and Abundance
Live a Life of Vision, Purpose, and Fulfillment

With persistence comes success. You must persist no matter how slow you have to move at first. No one enjoys great achievement without passing the persistence test. Those who can endure are greatly rewarded for their persistence. They receive as their reward, whatever goal they are pursuing.

Lack of persistence is one of the greatest causes of failure. You must labor. You must endure. You must ignore the obstacles at your feet and keep your eyes on the goals in front of you. You may still encounter failure, yet success hides behind the next corner. Strain your potential until it cries for mercy.

Dream big dreams! Reach for the moon, and even if you miss, you will land among the stars! It is better to attempt to do something great and fail, than attempt to do nothing and succeed.

Before success comes in your life, you will meet with temporary defeat and even some failure, but success will come just one step beyond that point at which momentary defeat tries to overtake you. Temporary defeat is NOT permanent failure!

A very large portion of your success will come from eating the bread of adversity, and drinking the waters of affliction.

IMPOSING ON THE MEETING

When I joined the Master Mind Women's Group (MMWG), it was totally by mistake in the natural eye, but it was orchestrated by God for His purpose. I went to the home of Ann McNeil for a college alumnae meeting that she was conducting. When I arrived, the meeting had already started, or so I thought. I pulled up a chair and joined the women who were already sitting and talking. I listened as one lady, Juanita, was' giving her report. She was talking about the goals that she had set and the progress she had made toward the attainment of her goals. She began reporting in different areas of her life. She talked about what she was doing to keep her relationship with the Lord progressing, what she was doing health wise, the books she was reading, etc. After she finished her report, there were some questions asked by the other members relative to her goals and suggestions were made on how she could improve areas that she had been struggling in. It was as though she had to give an account of what she had previously told them relative to her goals. After her report was completed, another member began giving a report on the progression of her goals. While sitting there, I realized that I was in the wrong meeting, but I was too embarrassed and too interested to get up and leave. It would have been too obvious. After the meeting was over, Nifretta, a member of the MMWG, approached me and introduced herself. She handed me a book and said, *"This is the book that we are reading for the month, and these are the forms that we are using to write our goals."* She was very nice as she was giving me all the information, and she welcomed me to the group as though I was a new member. I went to Ann and apologized. I explained to her that I did not mean to impose on her meeting, but I thought that it was the alumnae meeting. I proceeded to tell her that Nifritta thought I was a new member and had given me a book and other information. I told Ann that I was very interested in becoming a member and wanted to know if and how I could become a member of the MMWG. Needless-to-say, she welcomed me with open arms and told me that all I needed to do was read the book that I was holding in my hand, which was, *Think and Grow Rich* by Napoleon Hill. She told me that after I read the book, I needed to give a report at the next meeting on how I will apply the principles to my life. I became a member of the MMWG, and I read every book that was required of me. I developed my personal affirmation, began setting my goals and gave a great report at every meeting. I was so motivated by being in Master Mind, and as a result, I have developed and achieved many goals that I never thought possible. I attribute my humble success to that group, headed by Ann McNeil. Had Ann not talked to me about the importance of goal-setting and planning, I may have been haphazardly doing things in my life that have little meaning. Master Mind has blessed me immensely and still is today. I am constantly working towards achieving my goals and setting new ones to replace the ones achieved. The women in Master Mind planted the seed in me to write this book. After reading many motivational books required by the group, I put together and gave each member a motivational packet consisting of excerpts from different books we had read. Someone suggested that I write my own book from those excerpts and everyone else agreed. The seed was cultivated, watered, and nurtured, and your hands now touch the manifestation of the seed.

WHAT ARE YOU WAITING FOR?

Take a moment to ask and answer these questions:
What is one major goal that you always wanted to accomplish
and never did? What would it take for you to start working
towards that goal right now? What are the obstacles stopping
you? Can the obstacles be overcome so that you may pursue this
goal? Why haven't you done it yet?

I had you ask yourself those questions because I had to
ask myself the same questions regarding my life. I seriously
reflected on where I use to be, where I am now, and where I
want to be in the future. We have all heard the saying, *"You can
be anything you set your mind to be."* But how many people take
that literally to heart? I do believe that if your mind can conceive
it and your heart can believe it, then you *can* achieve it. How
many times have you pondered on something you have always
wanted to do, but never did? When that thought comes to mind,
do you feel bad or guilty about not having achieved it? Why do
you think you keep having thoughts and visions of it? The vision
has been imprinted in your spirit for a reason. The desire in you
is the power seeking to manifest. You are walking around with
seeds of God's purpose inside of you, and you are not cultivating
the seeds, nurturing the seeds, or watering the seeds so that they
can grow and blossom. Why are you hiding your gifts from the
world? It is not too late to go after that goal. Let's take an
example. If I wanted to become a lawyer, could I pursue that
goal right now? Would it be too late this far in the game? No. If I
pursued becoming a lawyer today, I would need to earn the
undergraduate degree, get accepted into a law school, study very
hard, sacrifice sleep, pass the Bar Exam, and eventually become
an excellent lawyer (I'm always winning arguments). Sounds
easy? I know there is so much more in between, but my point is
that whatever you want to do in life can be done with the start of

a goal and the necessary steps taken to achieve that goal. Big accomplishments are only but a bunch of small accomplishments multiplied. It is very sad to have lived forty, fifty, sixty, or even seventy years on I coulda... shoulda... woulda.. Time is waiting for no one. If you desired to go back to school to earn that college degree you always wanted, what is stopping you? Your age? Okay let's say you are forty years old right now, but you say that you are too old to go back to school. It would take four years to earn a Bachelors degree, two years after for a Masters (with these accelerated programs, maybe less than that), and three years minimum thereafter for a Doctorate, but you decide not to go back at all. In four years, you will just be four years older *without* that degree, but in the same educational position you were in four years prior; whereas had you gone back to school, you would be four years older *with* that college degree, a sense of achievement, and an increased level of self-confidence. How old we are is not important. It is one's view towards age that makes it a blessing or a hinderance. Stop thinking, *"I should have done that years ago."* That is failure thinking. Instead think, *"I am going to start right now because my best years are ahead of me."* My point is that no matter what age you are or what your present circumstances may be, you are never too old to accomplish your dreams. You are special and still have something unique to offer. Your life, because of who you are, has meaning. When you multiply tiny bits of time with tiny bits of effort, you will find that you can accomplish magnificent things. It is never too late to do anything you purpose in your heart and mind to do. Your sacrifice of time and effort should serve the vision that God has given to you.

God outlined all throughout the Bible what we needed to do to be successful. We just don't apply the principles to our lives. A good example of how God outlined success for us is in the book of Joshua, Chapter 1:8 *"This book of the law shall not* depart out of thy mouth; but thou shall meditate therein day and night, that thou mayest observe to do according to all that is written therein: For then thou shalt make thy way prosperous, and then thou shalt have good success." Good success is attaining total peace and fulfillment in every area of your life. God plainly told Joshua how he and the Israelites could have not just success, but "good success" and be prosperous. He said for them to meditate on the Word day and night and do what the Word says. Seems simple enough right? Then why was it so hard to do, and still is today? Because it takes discipline to meditate on the Word of God day and night. It takes discipline to *"do according to ALL that is written therein..."* It takes discipline to do anything that is worth something. Unfortunately, most of us keep our lives so jammed with junk food for the soul and amusement for the flesh, that the cost for good success and prosperity is too expensive for us to pay. God reiterates this same principle in Psalm 1:2, *"his delight is in the law of the Lord and in his law does he **meditate day and night**; and he shall be like a tree planted by the rivers of the water that bringeth forth fruit in his season; His leaf also shall not wither, and whatsoever he doeth shall prosper."* There it is again. God says to meditate on His Word day and night and we shall be prosperous. Prosperity is an ongoing, progressing state of success. God wants us to have prosperity and have "good successes," and He told us what we needed to do to have it. You can have it. I can have it. Discipline and obedience is the key.

THE EFFECTS OF LOW SELF-ESTEEM

Self-esteem refers to how you feel about yourself on the inside. The thoughts and feelings you have regarding yourself may be positive or negative. The more positive your thoughts and feelings about yourself are, the higher your self-esteem will be. On the contrary, the more negative your thoughts and feelings about yourself are, the lower your self-esteem will be. Feeling good, no, feeling great about yourself is imperative, as it gives you a sense of power over your own life, helps you feel satisfied in relationships, allows you to set realistic expectations, and enables you to pursue your *own* goals. Notice I said "own" goals. I place emphasis on this word because it is so important. One main characteristic of those with low self-esteem is that they go over and beyond to help others achieve their goals and seldom work on achieving their own. They do this so that they will be accepted, so people will appreciate them, recognize them, and praise them for their efforts and hard work. Yet, they leave their own goals and dreams on the backburner and never get around to pursuing them because they are constantly helping others fulfill theirs. Feeling good about yourself gives you that motivation required to achieve goals and reach dreams. Feeling bad about yourself, on the other hand, contributes to a distorted view of yourself and a distorted view of others. The limitations that you think you have, and the negative thoughts that you internalize are given to you by the world, but the possibilities that you envision for yourself come from within you by the spirit of God residing in your soul. Ralph Waldo Emerson states, *"What lies behind us, and what lies before us are tiny matters compared to what lies within us."* What a profound statement! There is so much greatness within us! Therefore, in order to be great, you must believe that you are great, expect great things in your life and be ready to receive them when they arrive.

People are looking at you and wondering if you truly believe in your vision, your goals, and your dreams. If you are not positive, if you are not confident, if you are not excited about your OWN dreams, how can you expect anyone else to be excited about your dreams? When you work with diligence towards your dreams, people notice, and they will support your vision. Everything you do will make an impression on others, good or bad. Therefore, it is of the utmost importance that we begin to value ourselves as individuals worthy of accomplishing great things.

One with a low self-esteem does not have the inner strength and fortitude to develop goals and pursue them with persistence and unwavering faith. Think about it. Is it characteristic for a person with low self-esteem to believe in himself or herself and pursue his or her goals? No, it is not. It may sound harsh, but unfortunately, it is true. He or she is too insecure and deep down inside they believe that they are not worthy enough to be great, although he or she may dream of greatness. If one asks for success, but prepares for failure, they will get the thing they have prepared for.

BELIEVE IN YOURSELF

There is power in believing in yourself. According to Les Brown, a man who had to dig deep within himself to find the value that he possessed, *"When people have a sense of their self-worth, a sense that there is greatness within them, the payoff comes in the increased value they place on their own lives and the lives of others. They are more likely to have an agenda for their lives, a mission that keeps them focused and shields them from the distractions and peer pressures that knock others off course."* Success in this life is not determined so much by the size of one's bank account as it is the size of one's belief. If you really believe that you can move a mountain, you can. But you must believe, really believe, and do not doubt. When you begin to have strong belief in yourself, your mind will start formulating ways to help you achieve your goals and your dreams. When you have a high level of self-confidence, others will have confidence in you as well. Once we have accepted and love who we are, recognized the gifts that God has placed in us, and walk in the belief, confidence, and knowledge that we are worthy of pursuing our dreams, we will never expect anything less out of life.

GOAL SETTING

You only get out of life what you invest in it. I once read that only 3% of Americans develop goals and strive to achieve them. Three percent! More often than not, people with goals and plans succeed in life, while people without them fail. If you have no goals to strive for and no plans for improving yourself, then what are you living for? This is certainly not to say that people cannot be successful if they do not develop goals, but life is much more meaningful when you are always striving to grow and working toward a goal. It is extremely important that you begin to accept yourself as a person worthy of accomplishing great things. Goals are like a road map, they show you where you want to go and tell you approximately how long it will take to get there. Plans are the "how" of goal setting. Plans delineate the steps you need to take along the way to arrive at your destination. For you who are visual learners like me, you need to see things written down on paper. Not only does writing your goals down help you to see clearly what it is that you aspire, but seeing them written down motivates you. Once you have taken the time and effort to write specifically what you want to achieve, the desire to accomplish those goals emerge from within you. There is power in writing things down on paper. The Bible puts it this way: *"Write the vision, and make it plain upon tables, that he may run that readeth it. For the vision is yet for an appointed time, but in the end it shall speak, and not lie: though it tarry, wait for it; because it will surely come, it will not tarry."* (Habakkuk 2:2). There is a resurgence of taking on the world that overwhelms you once you see your vision on paper.

However, once you get your goals down on paper, you must not file them away, never to look at them again. Spend time examining and memorizing your goals. Do not let the motivation die. If the obstacles that I have overcome are not enough motivation for you, then read the words of Les Brown, who states the following in 'Live Your Dreams', *"With a powerful hunger for your dreams driving you, you will be surprised at the ideas that will come, at the people you will be able to attract, at the opportunities that will unfold. You will be able to see things that you won't believe you couldn't see before – things that may have been right there in front of you the whole time."* You have everything you need inside of you to accomplish your goals. The only thing that can stop you from pursuing your goals is YOU! You are the master of your own destiny. You are the captain of your ship.

Properly setting goals can be incredibly motivating. As you get into the habit of setting and achieving goals, you will find that your self-confidence increases quickly. A sure way to increase self-esteem is by setting and achieving goals. Goal setting techniques are used by many successful individuals and achievers in all professions. Goals give you long-term vision and motivation. They focus your acquisition of knowledge and help you to organize your time and resources so that you can make the very most of your life. Cherish your visions. Have faith in your goals, for out of them will flow all delightful conditions and surroundings. Dream big dreams and as you dream, so you shall become. Falling into your hands will be placed the exact result of all your thoughts. You will receive that which you have created, no more, no less. Remember to dream BIG! Norman Vincent Peale said it best when he stated, *"When you affirm big, believe big, and pray big, big things happen."* Keep in mind that how big you think determines the size of your accomplishments. You are bigger than you think you are. People who dare to aim high and work towards accomplishing their goals are big thinkers. They are experts in creating positive, forward-looking, optimistic pictures in their minds, and in the minds of others. Don't concern yourself too much with *how* you are going to achieve your goals after you have written an action plan for reaching them. Leave that completely to God. Look at things not as they are, but as they can be. Visualization adds value to everything. A big goal-setter always visualizes what will be done in the future. A big goal-setter is not concerned with the present. The challenge of competing with yourself and winning is very rewarding. Don't give up. The reward is great if you persist until you succeed.

However you decide to plan is up to you. The key is to plan. When you fail to plan, you plan to fail. The majority of people meet with failure because of their lack of persistence in creating new plans to take the place of the ones that have failed. When they don't see instant results, they become discouraged and quit. There will be some failure, but that is okay. Temporary defeat is not permanent failure. It is in you to succeed. No one succeeds without overcoming obstacles and opposition. There would be no **test**-imony if there were no **test**. Out of every adversity comes an equal or greater opportunity. When setting goals, I always begin by defining who I am and who I aspire to be. I call it my personal affirmation. Others call it their mission statement. They are basically the same. I recite my affirmation at least twice per week. On the next page is an example of my affirmation:

Mia's Personal Affirmation

I Mia Yvette Merritt, am a prosperous, spiritual, humble, and faithful woman of God with character and integrity. As a child of the most high and powerful God, I meditate on the Word day and night. I pray without ceasing and I worship God in spirit and in truth. I exhibit a quiet and meek spirit, which in the sight of God is of a great price. I walk in this world with humility and grace, and yet I am confident and fearless. Out of my mouth departs wisdom, power, and the law of kindness. I control my emotions in every situation, I practice good habits on a daily basis, I attract and magnetize to me the people, circumstances, money, and conditions that I require in order to fulfill and achieve my highest ideals. I am great! I come from greatness! I attract greatness, and I am the kind of person I want to attract into my life.

I am a lender, not a borrower. I am above and not beneath. I am the head and not the tail. It is my birthright to live in prosperity, peace, harmony, and abundance and my life is a reflection of that birthright. I speak with perfect self-expression and my words rapidly perform those things which I speak.

I keep my mind, my spirit, and my soul healthy by reading books that feed me in an effort to increase in knowledge, wisdom, and understanding. All of my positive thoughts are being established. My daily mindset is one of constructive thinking, ingenuity, and absorbing the power and wisdom of the mind Christ.

As a mother, sister, friend, and wife, I encourage, uplift, and speak life into the situations of others, and bless them with the fruit of my lips. I speak what the spirit of God gives me to speak, and I do it in season, and in love. My children arise and call me blessed; and my husband also, and he praises me. Favor is deceitful, and beauty is vain, but a woman who loves the Lord, she shall be praised!

PLAN FOR PROSPERITY AND ABUNDANCE

Yes, my affirmation is long, but since I recite it at least twice per week, I cover every aspect of my life. Words have power and as I speak into the atmosphere, my words manifest themselves in the earth realm and return back to me with astounding accuracy. You should want all of your desires to come into fruition. Speak it into existence!

An affirmation/personal mission statement is basically a snapshot of how you see yourself in the very near future. Some people have much shorter ones, some have longer, but what is most important is to have one. Once written, you are consciously aware of the person you aspire to be, and therefore are compelled to begin acting like that person. It is so real. From your affirmation/mission statement, come your goals. Every year, I set goals in various areas of my life: spiritually, financially, educationally, recreationally, personally, family, business wise, and health. Many people set goals in only a few areas, but as I stated earlier, I like to have all areas of my life covered. Below is a brief example of how I set my goals:

SPIRITUAL GOALS
- Become more sensitive to the voice of God through prayer, fasting, praise and worship.
- Rise no later than 4:30a.m daily to pray and read the Word.
- Meditate on *at least* one Bible scripture per day.
- Sow into the kingdom of God by giving 12% tithes instead of 10%
- Give a monthly "sacrificial" offering.
- Fast at least twice per month to hear the voice of God concerning my life.

FINANCIAL GOALS
- Pay off at least half of my student loans
- Save $30,000.00 in checking account
- Pay off all credit cards
- Purchase at least five stocks
- Renew membership with the Chamber of Commerce
- Renew membership with International Mastermind Association.

PERSONAL GOALS
- Speak positive in all manner of conversation. Eliminate vain talk and gossiping
- Meditate daily
- Learn a minimum of 20 sentences in Spanish
- Maintain my nails and hair twice monthly
- Do 55 sit-ups a night
- Write and publish my second book
- Book at least three speaking engagements per month
- Send birthday cards to friends and family
- Tell my son that I love him every day
- Do at least one random act of kindness every week
- Call Grandma more often

EDUCATIONAL GOALS
- Learn to speak Spanish fluently
- Increase my vocabulary and enunciation
- Reinforce learned skills with my son
- Renew my teaching contract with the university

FAMILY GOALS
- Invite at lease 10 people to church
- Organize monthly family outings
- Have Sunday dinners at my home
- Take Stephan on a summer vacation
- Visit Grandma in Madison, FL
- Go to the movies and/or a concert or play at least 3 times with family and friends.
- Go bowling with nieces and nephews

HEALTH GOALS
- Take multivitamins
- Drink at least 3 pints of bottles of water daily
- Get annual physical
- Lose 5 inches around my waist
- Get a mammogram
- Take Stephan for his dental appointment
- Take Stephan for his eye appointment
- Take Stephan for his annual physical
- Exercise at least four times per week

CHECK AND BALANCE

As mentioned previously, your motivation is increased when you write your affirmation/personal mission statement. Writing an affirmation is time consuming. It requires you to look deep inside yourself and identify your strengths and weaknesses. Going deep inside and bringing out the less attractive stuff can be a humbling, yet beneficial and worthwhile undertaking. It requires soul-searching. Write down your strengths and weaknesses. However, after writing your affirmation, your yearly goals will be a bit easier to develop. Learn yourself and write down what you find out. Then, identify what you want out of life and what role you want to play in the lives of those whom you love and interact. Your motivation increases after you actually sit down and write out your goals. Your goals must be clearly defined, realistic, meaningful, and acted upon. In an effort to assist in the most important areas of my life, I use a Goals Form when developing one-year goals, (see p. 179 in back). Once the mission statement and goals are written, there must be accountability. Therefore, I use monthly and weekly forms as a check and balance system (see p. 182 in back). Every month I look at the goals that I have developed for that particular year. I then look at the smaller goals that I need to achieve in order to reach my large-scale goals. In doing this, I identify what is realistic enough to accomplish within a month's time. They are then written on the monthly form. Everyday, I look at the form and check off what has been done for the day. This next part may sound crazy, but at the end of the   month I calculate the difference between the goals accomplished and the goals not accomplished. I then take out my grading scale and give myself a grade – the grade that I earned (this comes from the teacher in me). I write my grade at the top of the form, just as if I am grading an assignment. I do this on a monthly basis. It is a (sometimes sad) reality check. I am pleased to say however, that I have never gotten an "F", but I have gotten a few "Ds", but mostly "Bs" and "Cs". I am, however, steadily moving and striving for "As." Goal-setting may sound like a lot of work, but nobody is going to put more time into your goals than you are. When you want success bad enough you must be willing to pay your dues to achieve it. Taking the easy way is the surest way to be misled. In all human affairs there are efforts and there are results, and the strength of the effort is the measure of the result. Nobody cares as much about your life as you do. Remember that.

FEAR OF FAILURE & FEAR OF SUCCESS

Psychologists say that all humans are born with only two types of fear: the fear of falling, and the fear of loud noises. All other fears are learned. They come with knowledge or develop as a result of our experiences. They come from what we are taught or what we hear and see. In his book *The Magic of Thinking Big*, David Schwartz, Ph.D, writes on the subject of fear, the following:

Fear is real, and we must recognize it exists before we can conquer it ... Fear stops people from capitalizing on opportunity; fear wears down physical vitality; fear actually makes people sick; causes organic difficulties, shortens life; and closes your mouth when you want to speak ... Action cures fear. Indecision and postponement fertilize fear ... Hesitation enlarges and magnifies fear ... To overcome fear, act. To feed fear, wait, put off, postpone ... the only cure for fear, is action.

Oftentimes the only thing that holds us back from accomplishing great things is our fear – fear of failure, fear of what people might say or think, fear of how we are going to make it financially, and believe it or not, fear of success. When you overcome your fears, great and mighty things begin to happen for you. The most liberating, yet surprising thing about fear is that when you finally do overcome your them, you realize that they were not as big as you made yourself think they were. I once saw an acronym for the word fear that is so very fitting: **FEAR=F**alse **E**xpectations **A**ppearing **R**eal. Once you overcome your "false expectations" and go after your goals with running shoes on, you will begin to do things you never imagined were possible. Fearlessness removes all fear. I am an avid reader, and I love reading old wise quotes, which is why I like the book of Proverbs so much, but one of the most profound quotes on fear that I have ever read comes from Marianne Williamson in the following. You probably have heard it before:

"Our deepest fear is not that we are inadequate. Our deepest fear is that we are powerful beyond measure. It is our light, not our darkness that most frightens us. We ask ourselves, Who am I to be brilliant, gorgeous, talented, and fabulous? Actually, who are you not to be? You are a child of God. Your playing small does not serve the world. There is nothing

enlightened about shrinking so that other people won't feel insecure around you. We are all meant to shine, as children do. We were born to make manifest the glory of God that is within us. It's not just in some of us; it's in everyone.
And as we let our own light shine, we unconsciously give other people permission to do the same. As we are liberated from our own fear, our presence automatically liberates others."

Whew! Talk about getting to the very heart of the matter. Can you imagine? Our deepest fear is that we are powerful beyond measure. Let's just overcome our fears and strain our potential until it cries for mercy.

MONITOR YOUR THINKING

We are all today where our thoughts have brought us and we will be tomorrow where our thoughts take us. Our character is literally the complete sum of all our thoughts. Your life is what you make it by your thoughts and deeds. You have no personality, no soul and no life apart from your thoughts. When you think, your life appears. As your thoughts are modified, you change. Your life cannot be separated from your thoughts. You have become what you are but are becoming what you shall be by your thoughts. You, and only you, can change your character. There are a plethora of books and materials written on the power of the mind, and yet scores of individuals still do not understand the power that their "thoughts" have on their lives, their experiences, their destinies. Life is about cause and effect, sowing and reaping, going around and coming back around. If you lie, you will be lied to; if you cheat, you will be cheated; if you give hate, you will receive hate; if you give love, you will receive love; If you give criticism, you will receive criticism. Wherever there is an effect, there is always a cause. To change the effect, we must change the cause and if we trace the cause back far enough, we will see that it can be found in the mental attitude which created the conditions. It is also important to note that effects become causes, which become effects, which then become causes. It is therefore important how we react to the effects. The person that you are today, the way that you carry yourself, the things that you have accomplished, the way that you speak, the job that you have, the car that you drive, all originated in your mind. James Allen, often referred to as an unrewarded genius, wrote one of my favorite inspirational books of all time titled *As a Man Thinketh*. The book is small enough to fit in one's pocket, yet powerful enough to change the world. The inspiring writings of James Allen have influenced millions for good and have brought fame, fortune, and happiness to those who have applied his teachings. In *As a man Thinketh*, James Allen writes: *There can be no progress or achievement without sacrifice, and a person's worldly success will be in the measure that he sacrifices his confused, evil thoughts and fixes his mind upon the development of his plans. The higher he lifts his thoughts, the more positive, upright and righteous he becomes, the greater will be his success and the more blessed and enduring will be his achievements.* Notice how success is contingent upon the way one thinks? To live, is to act and think, and to act and think is to change. Even if you are ignorant of this fact, you are still changing for either better or worse. We must become masters of ourselves because we have the power to control our thoughts. We must get ourselves right by monitoring our way of thinking.

When you find yourself focusing on negativity, which brings forth no good fruit, you must immediately switch your thinking to thoughts of a more positive nature. Once we begin to observe what we think about, we will discover that we oftentimes occupy our minds with petty insignificant details instead of letting it soar, as it was divinely designed to do.

Positive and negative thinking cannot occupy the mind at the same time. One must dominate the other. Therefore, it is your responsibility to ensure that positive thoughts dominate your mind. If you fail to plant desires into your mind, if you fail to focus on things that are positive and constructive, if you simply neglect to plant the seeds that will yield positive fruit, your mind will feed upon the thoughts that reach it as the result of your neglect. All that you accomplish or fail to accomplish with your life is the direct result of your thinking. It is imperative that you monitor what goes into your mind. You absolutely must change the programming of your mind, bring hope and happiness into your life, and awaken the faith and inner conviction that you can change, overcome, and improve any situation through your thought process. Thoughts of doubt and fear will never accomplish anything. They always lead to failure. If you allow doubt and fear to sneak in, then your purpose, your energy, and your efforts all become futile. Guard well your thoughts reader, for what you think in your secret thoughts today, good or bad, will eventually manifest into action tomorrow.

At the bidding of negative, disappointing thoughts, your body sinks into sickness and disease. At the command of pleasant and righteous thoughts, the body becomes clothed with youthfulness and beauty. Strong, pure, and positive thinking build up the body in health and grace. Out of a clean heart, comes clean thoughts and a clean body. To renew your body, you must beautify your mind. Negative thoughts of unforgiveness, hatred, and bitterness rob the body of its health and grace. Clean thoughts make clean habits. You must monitor your thinking in order to be truly successful.

NATURAL LAWS OF THE UNIVERSE

Regardless of who uses them, the natural laws of the universe cannot be broken. For instance, anyone who consistently gives 10% of his or her income to donations or tithes will have that money returned back to them in great financial measures. An atheist can apply this principle and reap the benefits just the same as a believer. This is the law of reciprocity. The natural laws work for or against anyone who uses them. People, in ignorance of the laws bring about their own destruction. Christians typically pay 10% tithes to their local church. Others pay 10% of their income to charitable organizations. The key is to give back a portion of what has been given to you. In life, we get by giving. We grow rich by scattering. Many have asked God to give them peace, righteousness, and blessings, but still have not obtained these things. Why? Because they are not practicing or sowing those things in their life. Since everything has a value, that which is freely given is gained with accumulation. If you were to read the stories of great financial giants, a common element among most, if not all of them attributable to their success is their monetary giving. My point here is that the natural laws of the universe do work when applied accurately. You may fail to observe the laws, but they are infallible.

There is the law of sowing and reaping and before you plant your seeds, make sure that you are going to be satisfied with what the harvest is going to be. Make certain that you are sowing the seeds that will sprout up good fruit, fruit of kindness, honesty, tolerance, wealth, time, service, etc. There is a time to plant and a time to reap. All of us have eaten fruit from trees that we never planted. It is therefore time for us to start planting seeds that will grow trees that will bring forth fruit that we may never eat from. Thoughts, words and deeds are seeds sown and by the infallible law of things, they produce after their own kind, good or bad. People may fail to observe these principles, but the principles are as mathematically exact as two plus two is four.

As you read this book, you might be in your reaping season. You may be in your planting season. You may be in your cultivating season. It is not difficult to discern what season you are in. You must know your season and continue working until harvest time. *"Be not deceived; God is not mocked: for whatsoever a man soweth, that shall he also reap. For he that soweth to his flesh shall of the flesh reap corruption; but he that soweth to the Spirit shall of the Spirit reap life everlasting"* (Galatians 6:7-8).

RESPONSIBILITY

With success comes responsibility. Through diligence, commitment, and a strong desire to succeed, many obtain success in this world. James Allen asserts that *some even reach lofty altitudes in the spiritual realm, but again, fall back into weakness and wretchedness by allowing selfish, arrogant and corrupt thinking to take possession of them. Your victories that are attained by right thinking can only be maintained by watchfulness. Many give way when success is assured, and rapidly fall back into failure.*

Knowing how to remain humble and keep a level head at all times will maintain your success. Pride is a terrible and dangerous condition to be in. It often is very difficult for the one afflicted by it to perceive it because it sneaks up on a person. The more successful you become, the more vulnerable you are to becoming lifted up in pride. The more prosperity you obtain, the more time you must spend with the Lord. Only He can protect you from the pride that has caused many to fall. The enemy wants to see you lifted up so you can you fall back down and be humiliated. Unfortunately, pride will not allow a person to admit that they are lifted up in it, thus making it difficult to get freed from it.

I once read a quote that stuck with me, and whenever I receive too many compliments from those whose credibility is questionable, I remember the quote: *Don't be afraid of enemies who attack you, be afraid of friends who flatter you.* Stay grounded. Be very careful not to get "caught up" in people praising and lifting you up. Remember, what the Lord said, *"No flesh shall glory in my sight"* (1 Corin 18:31). God alone is to be lifted up and praised. Stay humble. Humility is a precious and valuable attribute to possess. In heaven, the more humble you are, the higher your position. The world says that the greatest one among you should be served. God says the greatest one among you should be your servant (Mathew 23:11). Greatness is measured by service, not status. Real success is found while bowing at the feet of others. If you stay at the feet of Jesus, you will remain humble. In discussing pride and arrogance with my mother one day, she said the following to me that really stayed in my spirit: *"The feet that you step on to get to the top, may be connected to the butt you have to kiss on your way back down to the bottom."* Man will lift you up on a pedestal today and throw you away like yesterday's garbage tomorrow. How can you face people whom you have mistreated once you have been regimented, demoted, downgraded, and no longer respected? When you mistreat or overlook people because they are "beneath" you, they wait for your downfall and then rejoice when it happens. You may be the most knowledgeable, competent, and experienced person that has ever held the position, but if you treat people like crap, they won't care about your skills or abilities. Many people get caught up into thinking that they are indispensable and can not be replaced. To get an understanding of just how much you will be missed if you were to leave that position, read the poem on the next page.

Sometime when you're feeling important;
Sometime when your ego's in bloom;
Sometime when you take for granted,
You're the best qualified in the room.

Sometime when you feel that your leaving
Would fill an unfillable hole;
Just follow this simple instruction,
And see how it humbles your soul.

Take a bucket and fill it with water,
Put your hand in it up to the wrist;
Pull it out and the hole that's remaining,
Is a measure of how you'll be missed.

You may splash all you please when you enter,
You can stir up the water galore;
But stop and you'll find in a minute,
That it looks quite the same as before.

The moral in this quaint example
Is to do just the best that you can;
Be proud of yourself, but remember
There's no indispensable man!
Author Unknown

This poem applies to everybody, not just the "little people" like me, but ALL! If you are humble and genuinely good to people, they will do everything in their power to support you and make you look good. It is important to care about people. When you take time out of your day to ask the least among you how his or her weekend went, that speaks volumes, not only to that person, but to God. Smile at people, be genuinely interested in people and stay humble. It will carry you a very long way.

~~ LESSONS LEARNED ~~

1. Once you begin setting goals and making plans to accomplish them, you will discover that you can achieve those things you never dreamed of. It all begins with a personal mission statement, then the setting of your goals.

2. The only thing that is stopping you from being successful is YOU. Once you believe, and really believe that you have the seed within you to be successful through goal setting, you are on the path that leads to prosperity.

3. Humility is the key to sustaining prosperity. Ask for humility so that you will always remain level-headed.

~~ REFLECTION QUESTIONS ~~

1. Are you monitoring the thoughts that reach your mind or do you feed off the thoughts that enter as a result of neglecting to monitor your thinking?

2. Do you have a mission statement for your life that you are striving to accomplish or do you live your life from day to day with no goals to strive for?

3. Do you really believe that you are worthy of accomplishing great things or deep down inside do you believe that you are unworthy? How will you convince yourself that there is greatness in you that needs to be manifested in the earth?

Chapter

9

Reflect on Your Deeds of Each Day
One bad Choice can Change Your Life

At each day's end, I will carefully examine the progress and problems of my day's journey, and this will create in my mind a diary for today, and textbook for tomorrow.

In the evening before I retire, I will review the words and actions of every hour of the day, and I will allow nothing to escape my examination, for why should I fear the sight of my errors when I have the power to admonish and forgive myself?

Perhaps I was too cutting in a certain dispute. My opinion could have been withheld, for it stung but did no good. What I said may have been true, but all truths are not to be spoken at all times. I should have held my tongue, for there is no contending either with fools or superiors.

Am I guilty of omission? Was there something I could have done to help someone or a situation, but I neglected to do so? Am I guilty of commission? Did I deliberately do or say something that was not appropriate, nor fruit bearing?

Let me review my actions. Let me observe myself as my greatest enemy might do, and I will become my own best friend. I will begin right now, to become what I will be hereafter. Darkness may fall, but sleep will not cover my eyes until I have reviewed in full the events of my day.

THE VISITS TO HOMESTEAD

When my mother would take my sister and me to Homestead to visit relatives, we would be so happy. My mother's two sisters and their children lived in the low-income housing projects down there, which was 45 minutes south of where we lived. We loved it there because we played outside all day and into the night and did what we wanted to do while there. My mother also had cousins who lived in the same housing projects, so it was like a big family reunion when we went. Our cousins lived literally doors away from each other, and we would go from door to door playing and eating food. We had so many cousins, so there was always someone to play with.

As a fourteen year-old girl, I envied the way my cousins were able to do what they wanted to do. They had no curfew, stayed out all night, sometimes even for days, did not have to complete homework, did not have to go to school if they didn't want to, and had no one really telling them what to do. They had boyfriends at eleven and twelve years old, and the boyfriends were allowed to spend the night with them. They had no discipline, no structure, no guidance. They used profanity freely around their parents, came in and out as they pleased and basically had it made in my eyes. Boy, how I envied that life back then. They did not seem to get in trouble for anything. When they would tell me about their lives, I thought they had it made. When I would say, *"Don't you get in trouble when you stay out all night?* Their response would be an emphatic, *"No! My mama don't care."* These were twelve, thirteen, and fourteen year old children.

On the other hand, I thought that my mother was the meanest mother in the world compared to the mothers of my cousins who lived in Homestead. We lived in the North area of the county where we were one of very few Black families in the neighborhood at the time. We were only allowed to play in the front or back yard when we went outside. If we did go to someone's house, it had to be someone on our block and my mother had to talk to their mother first. She would give us a time to be home and we had to be in the house before the sun went down or she would come and get us from wherever we were and embarrass us. We were not allowed to play with boys unless it was in the front yard where she could look out of the window and we could not spend the night at anyone's house. Girls could spend the night at our house, but I wanted to go to other people's homes and spend the night sometimes. When we came home from school, we had to do our homework and leave it out for mother to check. If it was not done correctly when she checked it, she would wake us up to re-do it. Boy, did I think my mother was mean. That's why whenever we went to Homestead to visit our relatives, Lisa and I would be so happy because we knew we were in for some freedom and some fun. There was always excitement going on in the projects - fighting, shooting, loud music, dance competitions on the basketball court, you name it. All the kids would be out late, even after 11:00 p.m. there would be children outside playing.

Boyfriends? Huh, I'd better not even think about having a boyfriend at fourteen. I did like boys, but they never knew it. I would always get nervous and shy around boys that I liked, so unless they approached me, I would never talk to them unless I did not like them. In that case, they were just my friends. My cousins had boyfriends, and they would try and set me up with boys who lived in the projects. I did like the attention. The only thing I did not like about going down there was when people would say that my sister and I talked 'White'.

MONKEY SEE MONKEY DO

I'll never forget this one particular time that we went to Homestead. We had been outside playing mostly all day. We were back and forth buying candy from the candy house, a place where this couple sold candy, chips, and soda out of their apartment. We had been playing all day long and going from house to house visiting relatives. On this particular day, I did not know where my mother was. When she would go to Homestead to be with her sisters and cousins they would hang out and she would leave us with our great aunt, a much older aunt, who let us do whatever we wanted to do. That was the only time my mother was not tight on us regarding our whereabouts. This particular day, I went to my aunt's apartment to look for my sister. I vividly remember walking into the house and seeing two of my cousins sitting on the couch with a boy beside each of them. There was a third boy sitting on the chair alone. They were all watching a triple X adult movie. The people on the tape were having sex. The first thing I said was, *"Ooh, I'm gonna tell!"* One of the boys asked who I was, and my cousin responded, *"That's our cousin, she's from Carol City."* He proceeded to say, "*What's wrong with her?"* and my cousin said, *"She square, they from a white neighborhood."* I closed the door and left. When I returned about an hour later, no one was in the living room, except the boy who was sitting in the chair by himself. So I asked him where everyone was. He said that they were in the back rooms. When I went to the bedrooms, my cousins were inside having sex with the boys they had been watching the movies with. One of my cousins was on the bottom bunk bed with a boy, and my other cousin was on the top bunk having sex with the other boy. I started yelling, *"Ooh, I'm gonna tell, I'm gonna tell!"* My older cousin, the one who was a year older than me, jumped up, started yelling at me, and said, *"Why don't you stop acting like a little girl."* By then, the other cousin had gotten up, and was a little calmer. She said that I should have sex with Ricky, who was in the living room. I exclaimed, *"I'm not doing that!"* The other cousin said that Ricky had told them that he liked me. Then she tried to convince me that sex was nothing, and that all I had to do was lay down and open my legs. She said it would feel good. After much debating back and forth, I was convinced to consider it. My cousin went to the living room and began talking to the young man about me. I was in one of the other bedrooms where she had told me to wait. I was so scared. I had never had sex before, nor had I ever seen a man's private part. As a late bloomer, I had not even had a menstrual cycle yet, and I was fourteen. Ricky came in the room where I was. He walked in slowly and said, *"You want to have sex?"* I said, *"I don't care."* Then he said, *"You have to take your shorts off."* I said, *"OK, turn around."* I slid in the bed and took off my shorts while under the covers. He began to take his shorts off as well. Then he climbed on the top of me and put his private part at the tip of my private part, but all of a sudden, a liquid came out of him before, we could do anything. He seemed to be afraid. I assumed that had never happened to him before, and I don't think that he had ever had sex before either. He did not know what the liquid was, and he never inserted himself inside of me. We both got up and put our clothes on. It did not work, at least I thought it hadn't.

A SHOCKING SURPRISE!

About four months later, my mother took me to the doctor for having stomach pains. The results came back. I was

161

pregnant! Needless-to-say, my mother was devastated. She became sick and desperate and didn't know what to do. She wanted to know what had happened. She knew that I wasn't sexually active, and she could not believe that I was pregnant. I was too far along to have an abortion and they wouldn't give me one anyway since my little body had not fully matured to that of an adult (back then, fourteen year olds did not look like 20 year olds as they do today).

She ended up sending me away to a home for unwed pregnant girls who gave their babies up for adoption. My mother told family and friends that I went to California to live with my father. I was actually right in Miami-Dade County. The plan was that I was going to have the baby, put it up for adoption and then return back home to the normal life of a fourteen year old. Informing the parents of the boy was completely out of the question. All that would have done was made me look like a fast girl and cause problems. The mentality of most people who lived in the projects during that time was apathetic and belligerent about everything except for drugs, sex, and welfare checks.

BYE BYE, MIA

So off I went to the home for girls. I was the youngest one there until a twelve-year-old girl came who had been raped by her stepfather. Shortly after that, an eleven-year-old came in. The home was very structured. We had three meals a day, home school, daily chores, and had to be in bed with lights off by 10:00 p.m. every night. We also took Lamaze classes three times a week. The only time we were able to leave the premise was on Saturdays, and we had to be back on the grounds before 11:00 pm or we would be penalized by not being able to leave the next weekend. I never went anywhere on weekends because I didn't have any place to go. All of my family and friends thought that I was in California. My mother came to visit me three times the entire time that I was there, and I received no other visitors because no one knew about the pregnancy.

I hated being pregnant. I would do things to try and have a miscarriage. I would do cartwheels, run, jump, and sometimes I would punch the area that the baby would move on. Why did this have to happen to me? I had never even had a menstrual cycle. I had never had sex before, and still hadn't! My medical file was proof of that. The very first time I went to the doctor for a check-up during the pregnancy, they were astounded. I remember my gynecologist calling other doctors in the room to examine me, and I felt so uncomfortable with so many people trying to look "examine" me. I remember one doctor saying, *"It's as though she's never been touched."* They asked me how I became pregnant because my body was that of a virgin. I explained to them that the boy did not enter inside of me, but that his tip was on the entrance of my private area. They were very cautious of my pregnancy, and also concerned that I wouldn't be able to have a vaginal delivery because of my fragile body. My pregnancy was always an issue with the doctors, and I had more doctor visits than the other girls because of it. I believe they were afraid that if something went wrong, they would be sued.

THROUGH THE WINDOW

The time came for me to have the baby, and I will never forget that day. I was lying on the bed watching *The Jefferson's*. When the show went off at 4:30p.m., I got up to use the bathroom when all of a sudden water came rushing down my legs. I notified the housemother on duty, who then notified the hospital, which was walking distance from the facility where I was living. They did not take me over right away. In fact, they made me walk around the premise, take a shower, and practice breathing exercises. Hours later, when my contractions were minutes apart, I was finally able to walk to the hospital with one of the housemothers. I had a normal vaginal delivery and the baby boy was born at 10:50 p.m. that night. I was not supposed to see the baby. After the birth, the baby was supposed to be immediately taken away, and I was to be taken to another floor. Obviously, one of the medical personnel did not know that because after the baby was cleaned off, someone wrapped him in a blanket and brought him to me. All of the hatred I had for the baby was immediately gone, and an overwhelming sense of love for that child was poured into my heart. He was a handsome little fellow with a head full of beautiful black hair. I held him for about five minutes and then they came and took him. I was taken to another floor and they never brought him to me again.

I would walk to the maternity ward to see him several times a day while I was still in the hospital. I would notice that all of the babies were positioned in front of the glass window for people to see them, but my baby wasn't. He was the only baby that was not displayed in front of the window. His little incubator was in the back of the room, so I would have to strain to see him. Once I was released from the hospital, I walked back there everyday to get a view of him. I would stare at him from the outside of the glass window.

One day when I was staring at him from the window, a young Hispanic girl approached me and began talking to me. She must have been about eighteen or nineteen years old. She obviously had seen the sadness in my eyes as I would stare inside the window. She approached me and was so gentle and sweet to me. She asked me my name, and after I told her my name, she said, *"Which baby are you here to see?"* I pointed to the baby that was in the back of the room away from the other babies. Then, she asked me *"Is that your baby?"* I shook my head yes. She said, *"Tell the nurse that you want to see your baby."* She proceeded to call for one of the nurses to come out, and she was very insistent. She said to the nurse, *"That baby in the back is her baby and she wants to see him."* The nurse opened the door and asked me to come in. My new friend came in with me. The nurse took me to an area away from the view in the window, and I was able to sit down and hold him. I was crying the entire time. My new friend was sitting next to me and holding my hand. I'll never forget that day, nor will I ever forget that young girl who showered me with love and compassion. I still pray for her today. As I write this, I pray for her that God would bless her wherever she is. I wouldn't know her if she was to walk up to me and ask for the time, but God knows who she is and I'm confident that he blessed her for her kindness towards me that day.

My mother came to the hospital after the baby was born. When she saw him, I believe that she felt the same love towards him as I did. She asked me if I wanted to keep him. She said that if I wanted to keep him, I could. I declined. I knew that it would be a hardship on her as a single mother, and me as a young girl. We would have had a lot of adjusting, not to mention explaining to do. I was fifteen years old by then, but I was wise enough to know that a fifteen year-old had no business having a baby. I needed to finish high school and try to live the life of a normal teenager. I could not take care of a baby, and it was hard enough on my mother having to take care of three daughters. She was newly divorced and trying to provide for us alone. It wasn't easy on her, and I knew that. I really believe that she wanted to keep him however.

The following day, I went back to the hospital to see the baby, but he was gone. I inquired as to where he was, and they told me that a social worker came and took him to a foster home. I never saw him again, but I did write him a letter, and my social worker assured me that he would get it.

A WISE CHILD

My mother and I subsequently had to go to court. I really didn't know exactly what was going on, but I knew it had something to do with "the baby". As we entered the courtroom, the judge ordered everyone out except for my mother, my social worker, and a few other relevant parties. He asked me a few questions such as, *"Are you giving up this baby for adoption on your own free will?" "Did anyone influence you to give this baby up?" "Are you certain that this is what you really want to do?"* When the judge was convinced of my answers, he gave the order and the adoption was executed. I had to sign many papers. I left the courthouse and went back home to my family. After we came home, my mother never brought it up again.

It's been over twenty years as I write this, and she has still never talked to me about it. Whenever I would try and bring 'the baby' up, she would discourage me from talking about him. So, from that time until the present, I have never had a discussion with my mother about 'the baby', whom I never even named. His birthday is on September 5, 2007.

I thought about "the baby" often. Every year on his birthday, I would secretly sing him happy birthday and I still do. I have prayed for him over the years and I often wonder what his life is like. I pray that he is an upright and decent young man who isn't a big problem for his family. I know that if I diligently sought him, he could be found, but I don't know if I am ready for that right now. The experience of having that baby is one of those deep dark secrets that has been tucked and hidden down within my soul. It has been extremely hard writing all of this down because it brought forth many memories that I had to relive. I have had to stop writing several times just to cry because facing the details surrounding that situation has been sorrowful.

NEW MERCIES

God gives us new mercies with each day. We all have made mistakes in life, and we all have done things that we are now sorry for, regret, or ashamed of. When we examine our deeds of each day, we can plainly see the error of our ways, and strive to correct from them. When we ask God to show us the hidden things that are holding us back or keeping us from being all that we can be, He will. When we truly desire to be delivered from everything that is holding us hostage and keeping us bound, He will purge, wash, deliver, and set us free. As we continue to examine our deeds, we will find the strength to turn those experiences into confessions in order to be able to bless others. You will be surprised at how many other people you will find with similar, if not identical stories. As we continue to grow in the knowledge and wisdom of God the Father, we will walk in righteousness, and the actions and deeds from most days if not all will be that of joy and peace.

I believe that we as humans, imperfect by nature are guilty of passing judgment on individuals just by observing their actions. We have no idea what people have been through and more importantly, what they may currently be going through. Many times, people act in certain ways because of some traumatic life-experience, brutal act, or other painful incident they may have undergone. The wound may still be in their heart tormenting them continuously. We must reflect on our deeds of each day and determine if our decisions will bring on consequences that will last a lifetime. A split second can change the course of your life and affect your destiny. Less than five minutes of experimenting with sex caused me a lifetime of deep impact. Before succumbing to temptation, look ahead to what the repercussions from the temptation could be, and then ask yourself the question. Is it worth it? Let the results of your daily examination be positive and pleasing. They should be nothing that you have to be ashamed about, but if they are, just remember that you have the power to forgive yourself and your Heavenly Father will always forgive you when you sincerely ask Him. Tough times don't last, but tough people do. Walk in wisdom. Examine each night your deeds of the fading day.

~~ **LESSONS LEARNED** ~~

1. Be obedient to your first mind. Second guessing yourself can often lead to regret, shame, and disappointment.

2. As children, we don't always understand why our parents seem so strict. It is not until we are older that we can appreciate the sternness. Strictness always seems like bondage, but the end result works out for your good. Freedom always seems like fun, but the end result is usually failure and disappointment.

~~ REFLECTION QUESTIONS ~~

1. What regretful decisions in life have you made? What is the goodness that you can find in that decision to help you move on, be strengthened, and grow?

2. Do you reflect on your behaviors and actions at the end of each day? Were there any decisions that were made that you can resolve before they get out of control?

Chapter
10

Pray with an Attitude of Gratitude
He Hears Your Prayers

I will pray for guidance.

Heavenly Father,
I come to you in humble submission to honor, worship, praise,
and magnify your holy and righteous name. I thank you for life,
health, strength, and the wisdom to know that you are to be
magnified and honored in my life. I thank you for putting the
spiritual strength and fortitude inside me, which has enabled me
to overcome every trial, tribulation, hardship and difficulty in my
life. Each encounter has made me stronger, better, and wiser.
Each victory has increased my faith in you to deliver me out of
every seeming impossibility.

Lord, please continue to teach me how to live this life with faith,
courage, integrity, grace, and confidence. Allow me a forgiving
heart and mind that will lead me on the path that keeps me free
and strong. Help me to always strive for the highest legitimate
reward of merit, ambition, and opportunity; but never allow me
to forget to extend a kind, helping hand to others who need
encouragement and assistance.

Lord, I ask for wisdom to acknowledge rewards and recognition
with humility. Let the spirit of excellence, understanding and
patience take
root in my heart, mind and soul manifesting through actions,
words, and deeds.

*Keep me forever serene in every activity of life. Allow me to
possess a tranquil heart that will keep me calm regardless of
unfavorable circumstances.
In sorrow, may my soul be uplifted by the thought that if there
were no shadow, there would be no sunshine. Steady me to do
the full share of my work and more with efficiency and
effectiveness, and when that is done, stop me. Pay what wages
thou will, and permit me to say from a loving heart, a grateful
... ...AMEN.*

GRATITUDE

I find it fitting for the last chapter of this book to be about
gratitude. Why? Because after overcoming many challenges
from my past, I am still here. I am still standing. I am still
healthy, in my right mind and I am grateful. Each day is a new
day, an unfoldment. The decisions that we make today
determines how and where we will end up tomorrow. If I looked
at the circumstances surrounding my past and sighed over them,
feeling sorry for myself and asking "why me?" and all the while
doing nothing productive to help get me through them, I would
never have ended up where I am today. Today, I am happy,
healthy, whole, strong, powerful, harmonious, loving, and
happy. I can see now, as I look back, how every situation made
me stronger. Each challenge awakened seeds inside me that grew
and blossomed into powerful testimonies, which has blessed the
lives of others. I don't regret a single experience. I am grateful
that God chose me to use to bring glory and honor to His name
through such challenges!

If we had no problems for God to solve, no difficulties to
overcome, no challenges to face, and no obstacles to cross, then
how would we know that God can bring us out, over, or through

them? When we ask God for strength, He sends us the difficulties which make us strong. When we ask for courage, He gives us dangers to overcome. When we pray for wisdom, He gives us problems that require wisdom to solve them. A very large portion of our spiritual growth and worldly prosperity will come from eating the bread of adversity and drinking the waters of affliction.

When we find ourselves giving thanks for EVERYTHING, we open a floodgate of blessings to come pouring toward us. We place ourselves on a current that draws good things our way. There is always something to be grateful for. I once read the following quote said by Buddha, which really sums up the fact that there is always something to be grateful for: *Let us rise up and be thankful, for if we didn't learn a lot today, at least we learned a little, and if we didn't learn a little, at least we didn't get sick, and if we got sick, at least we didn't die, so let us still be thankful.*

When my daughter died after having lived for only 93 days, I gave thanks to God for giving her to me for that period of time. She could have died at birth, and I never would have gotten to know her, love her, feed her, change her, care for her, but he allowed me to do those things, which I will always cherish in my heart. I give thanks.

PRAYING IN THE PRESENT TENSE

I find that when we pray as though what we ask for has already been received, the manifestation of what is desired comes faster. For example, if your desire is for a husband, your prayer should sound something like this: *Father, I thank you for my loving husband. I thank you for blessing me with a man who walks in wisdom, knowledge and understanding. He loves me dearly, takes care of our household and prays for us. Thank you for this beautiful man who puts you first and has truly taken his rightful place as head of the household. Lord, this man showers me with love and affection, honors me, and communicates with me lovingly and honestly. I thank you for sending this man to me. I am truly happy that he is in my life and I pray that you continue teaching me how to love, support, and honor him. I am grateful for my husband and I thank you for him.* Whatever you want God to bless you with, pray in the "present" tense as though you already have it! If it is right for you to receive it, it is right for you to pray for it. Your hands shall begin to touch, feel, and experience the manifestation of it through constant gratitude. Begin to *feel* the spirit of gratitude now. Your strong thankful emotion will draw your desire to you speedily.

As I look back over my life, I can't help but be thankful, humble, and appreciative for the many trials that God has brought me through. I know that there are many remarkable people who have surmounted challenges far greater than mine, but my struggles, my pain, and my sorrows are mine, and the magnitude of those trials caused me to be that much stronger in God and has allowed my intestinal fortitude to emerge mightily. All of us have a story to tell. YOU have a story to tell, and I believe that there is a book waiting to be written in everyone. Put God first, pursue your dreams, discover your purpose, monitor your thinking, and everything in your life will fall into place just as it should. Start living your dreams today because you, like me, are *Destined for Great Things!*

EPILOGUE

In the Foreword, I said that this book was written and completed in August 2002, but never published. At that time, it was not the season for me to publish and disclose this book to the world. It was a time for therapeutic healing for me. Expressing my difficult life's experiences in writing was needed for me back then. Since then, God has delivered me completely and blessed me immensely. Now is the season for me to make known the things that have been written in this book. The five years that passed between then and the time that I finally published the book has been years of reaping the seeds that were planted in prior years.

When I wrote this book, I had been a teacher for nine years aspiring to become an Assistant Principal. Now, as I write this book I am in my fifth year as an Assistant Principal and am now aspiring to become a principal. From then until now, I have earned a Doctorate Degree in Education, opened a Motivation Consulting Firm, teach college students at the local university, and have published a book, this book. My son, Stephan is nine years old and in the fourth grade. He is a pleasant and delightful little boy who is in the Gifted Program at school, plays the piano and chess, talks a lot and asks lots of questions.

Who would have thought that a thieving child, who had a baby at 15, barely graduated high school, and been to jail, would amount to anything good. My life is an example of how God can take a sinner like me, activate His spirit inside of him or her, and use him or her as an example of His great grace and mercy. When we truly surrender everything to His will, mind, body, soul and spirit, He will make us into what He has predestined for us to be. We all have the capacity to deal with tragedy in our lives. It is just a matter of tapping into the inner strength and fortitude that we were given by God. We must learn from every lesson, and strive to bring out the greatness that is within us. No life is without complications and failures. You must expect tough times. If not you, then who?

Just remember that life is 10% of what happens to you, but 90% of how you react to it. Every pain we suffer brings us nearer to the knowledge of divine wisdom. May the wisdom, knowledge, and understanding be in your soul and when you have found them, there will be a great reward, and your expectations will not be cut off. May God bless you abundantly!

SUCCESS VOW

Taken from Napoleon Hill's Book
Think and Grow Rich

I know that I have the ability to achieve the object of my definite purpose in life, therefore I demand of myself persistent, continuous action towards its attainment. I realize that the dominating thoughts of my mind will eventually reproduce themselves into outward, physical action, and gradually manifest themselves into physical reality; therefore, I will concentrate my thoughts daily upon the task of thinking of the person that I intend to become, thereby creating in my mind, a clear mental picture.

I will devote time daily to demanding of myself the development of self-confidence, and I will never stop trying until I feel that I have developed sufficient self-confidence for the attainment of my purpose.

I will succeed by attracting to myself the forces I wish to use, and the cooperation of other people. I will induce others to serve me because of my willingness to serve others. I will eliminate hatred, envy, jealousy, selfishness, grudge holding, anger, and cynicism by developing love for all humanity because I know that a negative attitude towards others will never bring me success. I will cause others to believe in me because I will believe in them and in myself. I can do all things through Christ who strengthens me.

-Napoleon Hill

About the Author

Dr. Mia Y. Merritt is a single, divorced mother of one son. She was born and raised in Miami, Florida and matriculated in the Miami-Dade County Public School System. She is an Assistant Principal, College Instructor, Motivational Consultant, and Author. She accepted Christ as her Lord and Savior at an early age, but developed an intimate relationship with Him in her late twenties. Her Christian walk has not been easy, in fact, it has been a struggle, but she walks by Faith. Her challenges and experiences in life prompted her to write this book. Through the book, she shares the trials, tribulations, hardships, and difficulties that have strengthened her character and made her a stronger person. Writing this book was a part of her healing. She knows that there will be more tests and temptations, but feels that she is strong enough to handle them with the help of God.

I thank you for taking the time to read my book. I pray that you have understood how my hardships and difficulties have made me a stronger person and have drawn me closer to God. But most importantly, I hope that you understand that you too, posses the inner strength and tenacity to overcome every obstacle in your life that will draw you closer to greatness.

You were created to praise and worship, and when you consciously decide to worship God, He will guide your steps so that you will walk on the path that has been predestined for you. Find your purpose and you will find fulfillment in this life. You are never alone. You are very precious in His sight. He wants you to live an abundant life full of success, prosperity, love, peace, and joy. With God, all things are possible. Just believe and receive.

Mia

Yearly Goals

Name _____

SPIRITUAL GOALS

1. _____
2. _____
3. _____
4. _____
5. _____

FINANCIAL GOALS

1. _____
2. _____
3. _____
4. _____
5. _____

HEALTH GOALS

1. _____
2. _____
3. _____
4. _____
5. _____

PERSONAL GOALS

1. _____
2. _____
3. _____
4. _____
5. _____

EDUCATIONAL GOALS

1. _____
2. _____
3. _____
4. _____
5. _____

RECREATIONAL/FAMILY GOALS

1. _____
2. _____
3. _____
4. _____
5. _____

CAREER/WORK GOALS

1. _____
2. _____
3. _____
4. _____
5. _____

Weekly Goals Form

(Taken from Yearly Goals)

_____Goals _____Accomplished _____Not Accomplished

Spiritual

1. _____
2. _____
3. _____

Financial

1. _____
2. _____
3. _____

Educational

1. _____
2. _____
3. _____

Health

1. _____
2. _____
3. _____

Family

1. _____
2. _____
3. _____

Personal

1. _____
2. _____
3. _____

Prayer List

1. _____
2. _____
3. _____

Books to Read

1. _____
2. _____
3. _____

Act of Kindness

_____

Books That Have Inspired Me

10 Spiritual Principles of Success Women *Victoria Lowe*

Acres of Diamonds *Russell Conwell*

As a Man Thinketh *James Allen*

Battlefield of the Mind *Joyce Meyers*

God Chasers *Tommy Tenney*

Greatest Salesman in the World Part I *Og Mandino*

Greatest Salesman in the World Part II *Og Mandino*

How to win Friends and Influence People *Dale Carnegie*

Invest in Yourself Dr. *Marthenia Dupree*

Live Your Dreams *Les Brown*

Love and Law *Ernest Holmes*

Matters of the Heart *Juanita Bynum, Ph.D*

Success *Glenn Bland*

The Lady, her Lover, and her Lord *T. D. Jakes*

The Magic of Believing *Claude Bristol*

The Magic of Thinking Big *David Schwartz*

The Master Key System *Charles Haanal*

The Power of a Praying Woman *Stormie Omartian*

The Prayer of Jabez *Bruce Wilkinson*

The Secret of the Ages *Robert Collier*

Think & Grow Rich *Napoleon Hill*

Thoughts are Things *Prentice Mulford*

Remember that you are:

Destined for Great Things!